THE
REAL
Benny Hill

THE
REAL
Benny Hill

MARGARET
FORWOOD

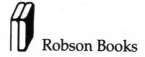 Robson Books

For Jenny

First published in Great Britain in 1992
by Robson Books Ltd, Bolsover House,
5–6 Clipstone Street, London W1P 7EB

Copyright © 1992 Margaret Forwood
The right of Margaret Forwood to be
identified as author of this work has been
asserted by her in accordance with the
Copyright, Designs and Patents Act 1988

**British Library Cataloguing in
Publication Data**
A catalogue record for this book is
available from the British Library

ISBN 0 86051 845 0

Filmset in Palatino by Selwood Systems,
Midsomer Norton
Printed in Great Britain by
Butler & Tanner Ltd, Frome and London

Acknowledgements

This book could not have been written without the help of many people, both in granting me interviews and in offering practical help, and I would particularly like to thank the following: Roy Addison, Annette André, Richard Brown, Bella Emberg, Louise English, Richard Flynn, Brenda Garrison, David Goodall, Tony Harris, Chris Hill, Philip Jones, Jon Jon Keefe, Jenny Lee-Wright, Melanie Louis, Bob Monkhouse, Victor Pemberton, Liz Roberts, Colin Shaw, John Spencer, Richard Stone, Don Taffner, Sylvia Thorley, Bob Todd, Peter Valvona, Tony Warren, Billy Whittaker and Mimi Law.

A special thank you to my editor, Louise Dixon, for her enthusiasm and her gentle handling of a novice, and to Laurie Mansfield who made me do it in the first place. And not forgetting D.L.K., without whom ...

Margaret Forwood

Foreword

I first met Benny Hill when, as a rather nervous TV correspondent for a national newspaper, I went to his London apartment to interview him. At that time, the middle seventies, he was at the height of his fame, in Britain at least; one of our best-loved TV stars whose shows went automatically to the top of the ratings. A large man, built like a teddy bear, he lived in solitary splendour in a huge and rather impersonal flat. But there was little to be nervous about. He was not grand or arrogant or difficult. There was no aura of self-regard about him as there is around so many stars of his stature. In fact, there was very little to set him apart from any ordinary man in the street, which is what he tried so hard to be. He was cosy company, full of old-fashioned courtesies. He had tidied up, set the biscuits out, put the champagne to chill and fussed around me like a fond uncle. He was at pains to be helpful – as long as the whole exercise was carried out on his terms. Benny did not suffer the Press gladly. Because his shows were screened spasmodically, rather than in a regular series, he appreciated that each one needed publicity to draw the public's attention to it, and endured interviews as a necessary part of the machinery. He prepared for them as professionally as he did the rest of his work. He would always have some anecdote, some new titbit prepared to provide a 'line'. He did not welcome those who went probing and prying and searching for their own sensational angle, though over the years many went along convinced that the oddities of his life-style must conceal something at least a little bit newsworthy.

The first few times I interviewed him, I got the impression of acting as straight-woman in a well-rehearsed script, being treated to 'revelations' so well-honed that he must have told them many times before. But eventually he began to relax and give me a glimpse of the warm, kind, rather eccentric man he really was.

He and I got on well, perhaps because I never over-stepped some invisible line between what he saw as legit-imate public interest in his work, and what he regarded as an invasion of his ultra-precious privacy. I was content to listen to whatever he wanted to tell me.

I have always been fascinated by comedians. Anyone who makes a career out of trying to make people laugh is halfway to being a hero in my book, and I can forgive them a lot of their other faults. But with Benny there was no real downside, no temperament, no self-importance, no lack of consideration for lesser mortals. He never talked about his achievements in a boastful or immodest way. He always seemed slightly surprised by the extent of his fame.

I knew him well, yet like many of the people I have talked to for the purposes of this book, I would never claim that I *really* knew him. There was an enigmatic quality about him. He often gave the impression of not really needing other people in his life. He was a loner by temperament, a charmer when he chose to be in company. It was difficult to dislike him. All he cared about was comedy, and he never let any conversation run on for long without trying to make you laugh. In fact, he would defuse any potentially serious discussion with a joke to the point where it seemed like an escape hatch.

I loved to watch him work. He did not really like to have outsiders around when he was making his shows, particularly journalists. He could not afford to break his concentration to keep an eye on what they were doing! But I was lucky enough to be allowed to go both to his rehearsals and his filming locations. And I must have passed some unspoken test, because it got to the point where he would be quite hurt if I failed to turn up one year, and would start asking where I was. We shared an obsession with TV – it was his life-blood. It not only provided him with ideas, he felt he was failing in his duty as a comic if he missed a single light entertainment show on British television.

Benny's real passions in life were comedy and the female sex and he managed to combine the two by studding his shows with pretty girls. Several of them became his closest friends. He had developed a near father-daughter relationship with one or two, but otherwise the girls' roles were mostly decorative. He never even came close to getting married. After his parents died, the regulars in his TV shows became his surrogate family. He called himself Uncle Ben, and they referred to themselves as 'the family'. He devoted himself to work to the exclusion of any real private life.

His working pattern was to travel the world for several months, both enjoying himself and observing the foibles of mankind, and jotting down ideas as he went, often sending them back to his TV producer written on beermats or cardboard shirt-stiffeners. As soon as he felt he had enough material, he would work on a batch of new shows for the rest of the year. Then it was off on his travels again, nearly always alone.

People to whom I described his way of life would often respond by saying: 'How sad'. But he was not a sad man at all. His life may have been solitary, but that was by choice. Because of his lifestyle, and his unwillingness to promote himself on chat shows and the like, he was dubbed a recluse. He hated both the label and the inaccuracy. When he decided to go out and enjoy himself, he did so with a will. When he didn't, he was never lonely. He was perfectly happy with his own company.

In Britain, he had been a TV star for as long as most families had owned a TV set. He was 'good old Benny', part of the living room furniture as much as the set itself. It was only when I travelled abroad with him, to Europe and to the States, and saw how he was lionized both by his fans and by his peers, that I realized just how much he was taken for granted at home. He was truly a megastar, but probably the most modest, unassuming megastar ever. He dedicated his whole life to making people laugh, and the world was a better place for his efforts. When he was sacked by his employers, Thames Television, after 20 years of faithful not to say financially rewarding service, the real reasons were hushed up. Benny being Benny, he meekly accepted his humiliation without any public protest. But he was never quite the same man again and I feel the story of his extraordinary fall from grace deserves to be told as it actually happened. This book is based on many conversations with those whose lives touched his. I cannot claim to give a complete picture of someone so very private, but I hope that the reminiscences of many of those who knew him will shed some light on the personality of a truly remarkable man. Any qualms I have had about undertaking this project about someone so dear, so soon after his death, have been partially allayed by those members of 'the family' who assured me: 'Benny always told us it was OK to talk to you.'

To them I am particularly grateful.

1

The End of a Legend

Early in the evening of the Bank Holiday Monday of Easter 1992, accountant Bill Greenham realized he had not seen his neighbour for a couple of days. They lived in adjoining flats in a pleasant modern block on the banks of the Thames, a few yards downstream of the weir at Teddington Lock.

The two-bedroom apartments, with views over the river, were worth around £150,000, but the occupant of flat No. 7 did not even own his. It was rented fully furnished by the year. The tenant's name was A.H. Hill, but he was better known as the comedian Benny Hill, and at that point in his career it was virtually impossible to quantify his fame.

His shows had been screened in over eighty countries around the world from Russia to mainland China, from Swaziland to Venezuela, from Iceland to Angola. He had been dubbed into almost as many languages, including Japanese, and in the United States, saturation screening of his shows five nights a week had made him a cult figure. Indeed, much of middle America thought that the chubby-cheeked comic, forever surrounded by beautiful girls, somehow typified the English way of life. He was currently the most famous comedian in the world, acknowledged by many as a genius on a par with Charlie

Chaplin. He was also a very wealthy man. But you would not have known it from his lifestyle. The flat was modest, there was no car down below, no driver, no housekeeper, no secretary.

Sixty-eight years old and unmarried, Benny Hill had no one to look after him at all, and Bill Greenham had been trying to keep an eye on him since he had come out of hospital three weeks earlier, without offending his neighbour's overwhelming desire for privacy. Even though he had been ill with heart trouble, no one had been entrusted with a key to the flat.

Now Greenham became anxious. He had not seen Benny, who normally bumbled in and out of the flat doing his own shopping and going for walks by the river, since Saturday at the latest. Nor had he heard his usual records playing.

He decided to telephone Dennis Kirkland, Benny's TV producer and closest friend, to ask if perhaps the star had gone away for the weekend. The answer was no. Benny had not been planning to go anywhere. Dennis had last spoken to him on Friday, and had telephoned several times since, but there had been no reply. Then he was unworried, assuming Benny was out shopping or on one of his frequent walks. But now he feared the worst.

A slight man with receding fair hair, Kirkland raced the two miles from his home in Hampton Hill in his battered old Cortina Estate. There was no reply when he rang the doorbell of flat No. 7. At 8.07 p.m., he phoned the police and then decided to put a ladder against the second-floor balcony outside Benny's living-room window and climb up. It was not easy: the ladder was rickety and he hated heights anyway.

He managed to clamber on to the balcony and peer in through the window. What he saw confirmed his worst fears. Benny was sitting upright on the sofa facing the TV set which was still on. Even from outside the window it was clear he was dead. By now Kirkland's fear of heights had completely overcome him and he was too scared to go back down the ladder. As he waited for help, the light began to fade. If he looked outwards from the balcony he felt dizzy. If he looked in the window, he could not avoid the sight of his friend. It was growing dark and the scene inside the flat was eerily illuminated by the flickering light from the TV screen.

Soon help arrived. Two uniformed constables from Teddington police station, PC Peter Valvona and PC Marcus Bass, drove up in a van. They went round to the outside of the building, and spoke to Kirkland. By now he had totally accepted that Benny was dead and he was getting more upset by the minute. When they saw how unsafe the ladder was, the two constables decided to leave him on the balcony for the moment and went inside the block. Valvona carefully broke the two-foot by two-foot panel of glass in the front door of flat 7, reached in and unlocked it.

While Bill Greenham and a couple of other neighbours waited outside, the two officers went straight into the living-room. A bleak scene greeted their eyes. Benny was sitting on the sofa staring at the main TV set. He was wearing a red and white striped shirt and blue trousers. His feet were bare. His legs were stretched forward slightly, as if, said Valvona, he had been thumped in the back, presumably a result of the force of the heart attack which had killed him.

On a table beside him were a couple of plates with half-eaten food, and two cans of fizzy drink, but no wine. The room was clean but terribly untidy. As well as the TV set which was on, there was another on the floor beside it and a pile of videos. A bookcase was almost entirely filled with video cassettes all labelled in Benny's rather untidy hand. Every surface was littered with papers. The main table in the living-room was piled high with correspondence and other papers. No one could have eaten from it. Somewhere among the papers was the contract for Benny's new series for Central TV. There were clothes everywhere, including dirty socks. Benny had been like a child who dropped his clothes where he took them off. There wasn't a chair which didn't have something draped over the back. There were jackets hanging over the doors. Drawers were half open. In one, the officers could see a roll of banknotes, probably about £3,000.

It had been a warm Easter weekend, with temperatures around sixty degrees. The central heating was on in the flat. Benny had been sitting there, unmissed and undiscovered for at least forty-eight hours, possibly longer. Time and the heat had taken their toll and Benny's face and body were bloated. There was absolutely no doubt in anyone's mind that they were too late to do anything for him. The first thing the two officers did was open a casement window leading to the balcony and help Kirkland to clamber in. He went over to Benny and spoke quietly, saying his own private goodbyes. He was weeping, deeply distressed. Then he pulled himself together and got down to what had to be done, helping the policemen work out whom to contact.

The officers followed normal police routine: they had to call either the person's GP or a police surgeon, to establish officially that the body was dead. They summoned a police surgeon. Everything had to be done by the book even when the answer was quite obvious.

Meanwhile, they made a quick search of the flat, and discovered that the rest of it was as cheerfully untidy as the living-room. Once again, every bit of floor was covered with discarded clothes. There were a couple of cheque books lying around, and several pairs of trousers had cash in the pockets but, apart from the roll in the drawer, there was no great hoard of money in the flat.

In the second bedroom, the bed was heaped with new shirts still in cellophane packets. The kitchen was littered with dirty plates and bits of half-eaten food. If you'd wanted to make a sandwich, said Valvona, you'd have had to clear a space on the work top because it was covered with the remains of previous meals.

Once the two officers had radioed back to Teddington police station to report in to the duty officer, other policemen began to arrive. Valvona had not asked for assistance. It was a perfectly routine call to a sudden death, and far easier to handle than some he had dealt with, especially with Kirkland there to help. But because a very famous person was involved, curiosity got the better of his colleagues. The duty officer from Teddington turned up and the section sergeant, plus a couple of other officers.

'At one point it seemed as if the world and his dog was there,' said Valvona. Almost but not quite literally. It became a bit of a joke at the police station afterwards that a police dog handler had actually attended the incident, with the excuse that he was giving another officer a lift. But at least he left his dog downstairs in the van.

Kirkland was still very distressed but trying to cope. He and Valvona pondered what to do about informing the next of kin. Dennis did not know exactly which of Benny's relatives might qualify for this, and how they might be contacted even if he could work out who to tell. 'I don't think he really knew any family at all,' said Valvona.

From the telephone in the hall, they called Benny's

agent Lynda Ronan, who told the police she was quite happy for them to treat Dennis as next of kin. In view of his loyalty and devotion to Benny over the years, it seemed appropriate and it made the formalities that much simpler.

Once the police surgeon had arrived and confirmed what everyone already knew, Valvona had to summon an undertaker to remove the body. By this time, the news of Benny's death had reached the media, and there was a film crew from Sky TV outside. When the undertaker arrived he was anxious that the whole thing should be accomplished with as much dignity as was possible under the circumstances. He did not want to take the body out past the prying cameras of the film crew, but there was no other way. And so Benny was taken to the mortuary.

Because Dennis was now officially regarded as next of kin, and no crime was suspected, all the cash and valuables, such as they were, could be left in the flat. All PC Valvona had to do was secure the premises. As he waited for someone to arrive to board up the hole in the front door, Kirkland made more phone calls. Eventually someone came to fix the door. Everyone was free to leave. About a dozen reporters were now outside the flat waiting for comments. Sometime after 10.30 p.m., PC Valvona locked the front door and handed over the keys to Kirkland.

It was a sad and lonely end for such a universally loved figure. Those who cared for him were haunted afterwards by the thought of him sitting there all alone. But in a way it was inevitable. He was essentially a solitary man. And he had died doing what he loved best: watching television. All he had ever wanted in life was to think of new ways to make people laugh. And to be left alone to do it.

*

Fairwater House was a third of a mile from Thames Television Studios at Teddington Lock, and Benny had originally rented his flat there in order to be close to his work, one of several ironies that dogged the final few years of his life.

He had worked for the company for over twenty years, and was often described by them as 'the jewel in Thames' crown'. His shows had been sold worldwide, brought them many millions in revenue, and resulted in them getting the Queen's Award for Export Achievement.

Their star was an enigma and it is doubtful if they knew much more about him than the average fan did. People described him as, 'Close. Very close.' Even the man who was his agent for over forty years admitted he hardly knew him. And since he gave away so little about himself, the myths and legends proliferated. He was a multi-millionaire, yet he was said to be so mean he travelled by bus and tube rather than take a taxi. His other home was sometimes described as a shabby council house in Southampton and he was reputed to take his holidays in Hornchurch. People said he looked like a tramp. He could look smart, but sometimes his suits were from Thames' wardrobe department, and his shoes were ancient boat-like brogues turning up at the toes. But it was the carrier bags that really caught the public imagination. Benny did all his own shopping, and was often to be seen walking around carrying cheap supermarket plastic bags. He even used them to transport his luggage when he went on his holidays. To Hornchurch ...

Benny hated all the lies and inaccuracies printed about him. Yet his lifestyle was so odd, the public was largely incapable of understanding it. He was pilloried for not fitting into people's popular preconceptions of how a big TV star should behave.

Benny neither sought nor needed adulation. When it came it pleased him, especially when distinguished writers like John Mortimer and Anthony Burgess declared themselves great admirers of his work. But he had no ego in the generally accepted showbusiness sense of the word.

His occasional displays of temperament were too mild really to be called that – more like small outbreaks of tetchiness – and only occurred when the incompetence of other people threatened his own perfectionism. They were nothing to do with any self-perceived status as a star. He did not choose to live like a star. He did not need people around him to tell him how wonderful he was. He did not particularly enjoy meeting people, and was totally happy in his own company. He lived in a world of his own and did not much care for people trying to force their way into it. His friendships were conducted entirely on his terms. You could go so far with Benny, but try to take liberties, and he froze you out. So he was dubbed a recluse.

He had no real interest in the money his success had earned him. He did not buy a mansion on the Wentworth Estate and take up golf. He did not have a Rolls Royce, a villa in Marbella, a secretary, a personal manager, or a press agent. He had not been married or divorced and did not pay alimony. He did not conspicuously support charities or fling his money around. He was generous with his thought and concern for others, but avoided the flamboyant financial gesture. His attitudes baffled people.

He had neither the desire nor the ability to explain his actions or his motivation. Self-examination was largely alien to his nature. But if you knew Benny, you accepted him totally. His oddities did not matter. You no longer questioned them. It was just the way he was. He was a shy, kind man, without a malicious thought in his head. When he did admit people to his home, he went to endless trouble to entertain and amuse them. He was very cosy company. He had none of the spite and jealousy so often associated with his profession and would never publicly say anything unpleasant about anyone. He had a way of rolling his eyes when a person he disliked was mentioned which was eloquent enough, but he never put his thoughts into words.

His greatest crime, in the late 1980s, though, was not apologizing for his humour. Much of his comedy was very clever, a lot of his ideas inspired; many of his sketches are small masterpieces of observation. His influences were the early cinema stars and the music-hall comics he saw as a child.

He also parodied his own profession in a way which was subsequently copied by dozens of other performers. But the overriding image his work produced could be summed up in one word: bawdiness. It didn't necessarily describe the largest or the best part of his output, but there was something unique about the atmosphere of his TV shows: a cheerful lustiness, the recurring theme of the twinkly-eyed man totally surrounded by pretty girls. 'The Benny Hill Show' had an aura every bit as sexual as a James Bond film, only with a smile on its face. The difference was that Benny didn't get the girl. But he had fun trying.

Since he wrote all his material, this image was entirely of his own creation. His attitude to sex remained much as it had been when he was seventeen years old, and the sexual content of his shows was probably largely on a par with the sex in his private life – more innuendo than actual substance.

At this point in the history of entertainment, films were so explicit that a major Hollywood production could sometimes be confused with a blue movie; television was awash with comedians who used images even more graphic than the four-letter words they employed; and some tabloid newspapers were not only publishing their own 'how to improve your sex-life' manuals, but exposing the private lives of the famous in such intimate detail that the revelations read almost like soft porn. But Benny Hill, for some reason, was the one who was forced out of business. A small lobby of other comics, feminists and industry watchdogs had somehow destroyed him. He never understood what he was doing wrong.

His enormous popularity with the public continued, but Thames reached the point where they decided that this could no longer be balanced against the mounting criticism and the escalating costs of his shows. Three years earlier, he had been sensationally sacked.

A sensitive and vulnerable man, described by many colleagues as 'too soft for showbusiness', he had been more hurt than he ever let the outside world see. It broke him. He used to say: 'I'll never understand it till the day I die,' and he didn't. He had no rancour, only pain. He was even prepared to swallow his pride, go back to use Thames' facilities to record the last-ever 'Benny Hill Show', one made for American consumption, and never shown in this country.

Perhaps Thames were gradually embarrassed by the all-too-obvious presence of the former jewel in their crown into realizing their error. After all, it was hard to miss his burly figure padding up and down Teddington High Street with his precious plastic carriers full of videos. Perhaps the climate was changing again. Most likely, the company had lost its franchise, become an independent producer and needed some product as internationally marketable as 'The Benny Hill Show'. A few months before his death, they had actually invited him to go back and work for them again. He said no. Eventually. But he did say yes to an offer from Nottingham-based Central TV, to make some brand-new, high-budget shows for them. It would be just like the good old days. Pre-production work had been due to start at any moment, and Benny had been as excited about it all as he was about his first professional appearance over fifty years before.

2

The Early Years

Benny Hill was born Alfred Hawthorne Hill on 21 January 1924. He had a brother, Leonard, two years older. A sister, Diana, came along nine years later. Throughout his youth he was known only as Alfie. The name Benny was adopted years later when he became a comedian and decided Alfie didn't have that certain ring about it. So he called himself after one of his heroes, comedian Jack Benny.

His father was also Alfred Hill. Born in 1894 in Leytonstone, London, he was the son of Henry and Sophie Hill, both the children of comparatively middle-class families but now living in straitened circumstances. They had cut themselves off from their respective families by marrying against their wills. In the course of a peripatetic life, Henry sometimes worked as a busker, performing in the streets dressed as a clown. His son Alfred was also 'in the business' for a while, leaving the family at an early age to join Fossett's Circus. Alfred's brother, Benny's Uncle Leonard, also became a circus performer, a high-wire walker, and was killed in a circus accident. Benny's father later moved on from circuses to fairgrounds, but by the time he married, was a respectable shopkeeper in Southampton.

If the love of the big top can be passed on genetically,

then in this case it was. Benny adored circuses all his life, from the famous names he saw in Britain to the tiny travelling troupes he loved to visit in the remoter villages of France and Spain. One of the joys of becoming an honorary uncle to half a dozen children in the 1980s was that it gave him an excuse to go to the circus as often as he liked.

Benny's mother was born Helen Cave. She loved music and singing, and the Hill house always had a gramophone, but the real talent on Helen's side of the family lay with her sister Louise. Benny's beloved 'Aunty Louie' had a powerful voice and frequently sang semi-professionally in Southampton. Benny believed she could have turned full professional, but she married and had a family instead. But there was always a special bond between them, and he used to go and stay with her at her home in Bexley Heath, Kent, till she died in her nineties. They used to sing along together and talk endlessly about showbusiness.

In the thirties, the Hills moved to Westrow Gardens, a cul-de-sac of newly-built solidly respectable semi-detached houses. By this time, they were a well-known Southampton family, with a large extended network of uncles, aunts and cousins, in and out of each other's houses all the time. Benny had a particularly warm and loving relationship with his mother. In the 'Omnibus' documentary made in 1991, he indulged in a rare moment of self-analysis. 'I think I probably loved my mother more than my father,' he said. 'I was closer to her than to my father, though I was close to him too. I cried buckets when he died, but not when my mother died. Perhaps I felt guilty for not loving my father as much as I should have done.'

Benny's cousin, Chris Hill, describes his Aunt Helen as

very 'with it' for her day, a jolly lady who would sing along with the popular songs. But like her son, in later years, she preferred her own company. 'I remember calling round there once when they were all out at work, or school or whatever,' he told me, 'and she said, "Oh it's so nice when they're all out and I'm on my own." She used to sit on the floor and read the newspaper. She was a nice lady, I was very fond of her. And Benny was extremely close to her.'

Brother Leonard was later to hint that something dark and emotionally damaging had happened to Benny, then known as Alfie, in these early years. In his book, *Saucy Boy*, Leonard claimed that the American comedienne, Phyllis Diller, a great fan of Benny's, once said to him: 'He was hurt as a child, wasn't he?' 'That's right,' Leonard replied. 'You see,' said Phyllis, 'the hurt is the grit in the oyster. It created the pearl of his comedy.' Whatever this was supposed to mean, Benny always described his childhood as very happy. He was an attractive, chubby little boy with cheeks like red apples.

The Hills considered being fat to be a sign of prosperity. His father's goal was a big watch chain over a big corporation of a stomach. If you were thin, it meant you were poor and undernourished; if you were fat, you came from a good background, you were doing well.

'My mother was a tiny woman, a lovely lady,' Benny told me, 'but my dad was a big, big man. We were a family of balloons. If we went out for a walk, and a well-fleshed girl went by, my father would refer to her as a "fine big girl". If my parents had seen some of the girls I went out with later on, they would have been horrified. Skinny models and slender dancers would not have gone down at all well.' The Hills were spared this horror, fortunately, because Benny never took any of his girl-friends home.

His cousin Chris confirms that all the Hills were fat. 'Big heads and big stomachs,' is how he puts it. 'It was partly hereditary and partly eating too much.' Benny's father reached twenty-two stone, as did his brother. Benny's weight never got much higher than seventeen stone but he had a constant battle with it because the TV camera added so much. During his adult life he shot up and down between seventeen stone and fourteen, depending whether he was writing, or whether he was actually filming the shows, with frantic bouts of dieting in between.

His best-ever weight as an adult was when he was in the Army. 'I went home once,' he said, 'and I was only thirteen stone. My father was horrified. "Look at this boy, you can count his ribs."' For the rest of his days Benny had to be content with being described as chubby, cuddly or roly-poly. His face was particularly round, and when he smiled, his cheeks looked as if they had been polished.

Following his father's philosophy, Benny's love of shapely women developed very early. He said that at the age of eight or so, he used to go to tea-dances on Southampton's Royal Pier where the music was provided by Charlie Poland's band. He would go up to young women and ask them to dance, and if he was very lucky his cheek paid off and some of them would take a turn round the floor with the beaming little boy. He claimed that he was just about tall enough to bury his face in their bosoms.

His main source of joy was that from a very early age he knew exactly what he wanted out of life, and never changed his mind. From the moment he saw his first stage show, he wanted to be a comedian. It gave him a direction in life. Chris Hill envied him for that. 'He was one of the few people I've ever known who did with his life exactly what he always wanted to do. Most of us have to adapt our ambition to what's available. He never did.'

His first visit to a variety theatre was to the Palace Theatre in Southampton, probably with his paternal grandfather. Chris Hill said: 'We all went with him to the theatre, though not all at the same time. We liked going out with him because he threw his money around. He was a dentist then, and he never had all that much money, but what he did have, he was quite happy to spend on us.'

Benny's parents also attended the theatre often, and he remembered having a regular seat from the age of about eight. He told me: 'I used to go to all the touring revues which would have eight, ten or even sixteen girls, plus a comic who was a bit Max Millerish and near the knuckle. There'd maybe be a baritone as well. And there was always a soubrette who played the French maid, in frilly knickers. And there I'd be, a little kid in short pants, looking at the comic and thinking, "Aren't you lucky up there!" He had everybody laughing and applauding him and about a dozen birds around him – who looked good from the front even if they weren't too hot from the back! I think my whole life was decided from then on. The shows I do for TV are the nearest thing on TV to a touring revue of the thirties.'

Benny explained he envied the comedian most of all because everybody loved him. 'He was loved by the audience, AND by the people on the stage, who often couldn't carry on for laughing at him. And I thought to myself what a great life.' He also claimed to have worked out at this tender age that the comic must be paid more than the rest, because he had top billing, something to aim for in

On holiday with his brother,
Leonard, in the early thirties.

The family home in Westrow Gardens, Southampton.

Form 2B, Taunton School, 1936 – from the attic of school pal, John Spencer. Benny is in the back row, far right.

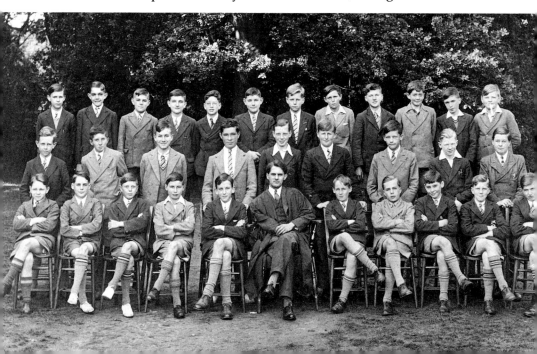

little Alfie's opinion. But the thing that made the biggest impression on him was really that the comedian was surrounded by girls. It was a motif that was to dominate his life, both on stage and off.

At this time his father was running a medical goods shop, selling trusses and surgical stockings and all the other things that used to make children giggle. But Benny got teased most at school because his father was the local source of contraceptives at a time when birth control was scarcely mentioned in respectable circles. 'Hilly's dad sells Johnnies,' they would snigger. It underlined what he was learning from the saucier comics, that a little sexual innuendo makes people laugh.

On Saturdays and during school holidays, Benny used to take his father's lunch to the shop, the dinner plate covered with another to keep the food warm. On the way he passed a couple of pubs where they had live music. 'It was usually nothing more than a piano and drums,' he told me, but it fascinated him. He never dared be late with the lunch, but on the way home he would dawdle by the pubs, putting his face as far inside the doors as he dared, to listen to the music.

His mother indulged his passion for entertainment, helping him to dress up as a comedian to make the family laugh. But that was not enough for Benny. By the age of twelve, he had acquired a few jokes and a guitar and joined an amateur concert party. And however amateurish his efforts may have been, he was set on a course from which he never wavered.

Benny used to fight a lot with his older brother. Whenever Chris stayed overnight at his cousins' house, he would be told to sleep in between the brothers in their large double bed. Mrs Hill hoped this would stop them fighting. Instead, it just ended up with Chris getting bashed from both sides.

Benny fought verbally with his father, who was known as the Captain because he always insisted on being in charge of everything. 'He was very abrupt in his manner,' said Chris Hill. 'I wasn't frightened of him myself, but some of the younger cousins were a bit in awe of him. I don't think he meant any harm, it was just his manner.' But Benny was always slightly nervous of upsetting the Captain.

One of the matters Benny and his father clashed over was Benny's schooling. He had won a scholarship to a good grammar school, Richard Taunton School, in South-ampton, but was not academically inclined at all. The only thing Chris Hill recalls him being good at was art. He could draw very well. 'And he once made a model of some famous statue or other, and the art master was really pleased with it.' Benny wasn't interested in keeping it, so the master took it home and kept it until his death. He bequeathed it back to Benny in his will. When his English master Dr King staged a play about a court case, Benny played a member of the jury and had only one line: 'Hear, hear!' But he said it with gusto. Even so, none of his fellows suspected they had a real performer among their number.

When war broke out in September 1939, Benny was evacuated with the rest of his school. Staff and pupils of Richard Taunton School were all moved to Bournemouth. On arrival, they congregated in a big hall, where the host families were waiting to collect the child that had been allocated to them. It was not as traumatic for Benny as for some of the younger ones, and in his case, it did not last too long. Benny did not believe he was getting anywhere at school, and later that year he left, without taking his matriculation. His father was not pleased but the boy was adamant. There was quite a family row about it. Nor was Alfred Snr pleased when Benny found himself a job as a clerk in a coal-yard office.

It may have been because of this row with the Captain that Benny left home at the tender age of fifteen, and moved into digs in nearby Eastleigh with a Mr and Mrs Brown. 'I used to get full board for a pound a week,' he told me. 'I also used to get clean sheets on my bed once a week, a radiator in my bedroom and good wholesome food. They were a lovely couple I lodged with. He worked on the railway and became a bit of a father figure, because I was so young and away from home. I'd be going round these Liberal Clubs and Conservative Clubs or whatever, entertaining, and they'd say, "Drinks for the band," and I'd say, "I'll have a sherry or a whisky. In fact, I'll have anything!" Once or twice I came home a bit the worse for wear, and the landlord was waiting up for me. He'd say, "This is not very clever, is it?" '

Benny's job with the coal-yard did not last long. He tried a new tack and became a trainee manager at Woolworth's, a grand title for a dismal job. His father had been heard to say that it was a good firm to work for, because your promotion depended on how hard you worked and not on whom you knew.

There was the manager, Mr Dean, who was 'very married' according to Benny. Then there were twenty or so girls, and him. They called him 'Sonny Boy'. Benny's job consisted of unpacking crockery, checking consignments, oiling the smooth wooden floorboards in the store once a week, and sweeping up. This unfortunately included clearing up anything left behind after various dogs had done their worst on the floor.

The girls used to tease him unmercifully. Woollies'

popular perfumes in those days were Evening in Paris and Californian Poppy. One day a twenty-eight-pound carton of Californian Poppy smashed as it arrived at the store. Benny was sitting in the stockroom doing consignment notes, when the girls burst in and poured the contents of the broken bottles over his head. He stank for weeks, he claimed.

Benny was interested in girls from a very early age. He had had several tiny sweethearts when he was at infants' school and now he started falling for girls all over the place. But often he was too shy to plead his own case, so he would ask Chris to do it for him. 'When he was about fifteen, he had his eye on one girl who worked in a shoe-shop. But he never had the courage to speak to her,' said Chris. 'So he wanted me to go and do it for him. I had to say something like, "I know someone who thinks you're lovely and would like to go out with you." I remember hanging around at the back of the shop till she finished work and came out, and then I spoke to her. I can't recall what she looked like, but I know she said yes. And I got money for fixing him up!'

Benny was not so successful with a girl who worked at Woolworth's with him. 'I was a bit sweet on one lady who was on the toiletries counter,' he said. 'They say a little humility is good for the soul, but whenever a dog disgraced itself, it always seemed to do it right by her counter. It's hard to be a knight in shining armour when you're cleaning up dog pooh.' With the sort of joke which would probably have been banned from his TV show, he sighed: 'Whenever she was on toiletries, I was on hardware.'

He was still only sixteen when he decided, once again against the Captain's wishes, to leave Woolworth's. His next job was immortalized in his 1971 No. 1 hit song,

Ernie. He became a milkman with Harry Hands Dairy. 'I was sixteen and I thought I was driving a stagecoach into Dodge City,' he would recall. A school friend John Spencer was astonished to see Benny driving the milk cart. 'I was walking along when I heard a voice call, "Hiya Spenny,"' he said. 'It was him, brandishing his whip on this milk cart. I said, "Hiya Hilly!" but I was thinking to myself, "what has the poor fellow come down to...."' We'd all been given to understand that he'd gone into the management side of Woolworth's.'

First he was the 'boy' on another milko's cart, then he became a milkman in his own right. He earned twenty-eight shillings a week (£1.40p) and paid a pound in rent for his digs. He used to go round on Saturdays collecting payment, and told me proudly: 'I had 300 customers on that round and I could look at each name and remember exactly what they'd had without checking the book.'

The women made him laugh when they came to the door. 'A lot of them hadn't put their choppers in, so they used to hold their pinnies up over their mouths as they spoke.' About forty-five years later, a woman stopped him at Waterloo Station when he was running for a train, calling, 'Yoo hoo, Benny, remember me? You used to deliver my milk.' He resisted the temptation to say that he didn't recognize her with her teeth in.

Much as Benny enjoyed the milkround, and grateful though he was for the inspiration it later provided for *Ernie*, it wasn't showbusiness. He was still entertaining in the evenings, and becoming quite well-known locally, but it was not enough for him. He knew that to succeed he could not go on doing it part-time. He decided to jump feet first into the deep end. He left his job yet again, sold his guitar, and set off, aged a mere seventeen, for London and the bright lights.

3

Breaking into the Business

Benny spent his first nights in London sleeping in an air raid shelter on Streatham Common. Armed with a copy of *The Stage*, he had tried half a dozen theatres for work, and had got as far as an appointment with the impresario Harry Benet for the following Monday morning.

After sprucing himself up in the gents' toilet of a Lyons Corner House, and donning a grey pork pie hat he'd bought specially, he presented himself at Benet's office in Beak Street, Soho. Something about Benny's gauche charm appealed to Benet. He gave him a job as assistant stage manager with a touring revue at £3. 10s a week. Sometimes Benny was allowed to play tiny parts as well as carrying out his stage managing duties. He was sure he was on the road to the top.

But by now he was eighteen, and somewhere on the road his call-up papers caught up with him. He became Private Hill of the Royal Electrical and Mechanical Engineers, despatch rider and driver mechanic. As a motorcycle despatch rider, he wore little round goggles which later resurfaced as the spectacles worn by his most famous character, Fred Scuttle.

Strangely enough, he never drove a car again after the war. Whenever a car or motorbike was used in a sketch on the TV shows, he would happily drive it round the set saying, 'Ooh, isn't this fun?' but he never wanted one of his own.

Army life did not have much to recommend it to Benny. He was homesick, bored, resentful of the way he was treated by the NCOs. He spent most of his war service stationed fairly uneventfully near Dunkirk.

When the war ended, Benny remained in uniform but under much happier circumstances. He managed to get a transfer to Stars in Battledress, the Army entertainments division which put on shows for the troops. His first part was in a musical comedy called *Happy Weekend*, followed by the role of comic and compère of a band show in Germany.

It was 1946 when Colonel Richard Stone arrived in Germany to inspect the Stars in Battledress. A comedy actor before the war, Stone had fought during the hostilities, and now at the age of twenty-six, was in charge of forces' entertainment productions all over the world.

Originally Benny was not due to appear in this particular show at the Shloss Theatre. But the local entertainments manager, Bill Day, had decreed he wasn't good enough. But sergeant in charge of the revue, Harry Segal, a professional entertainer in civvy street, heard that the colonel was in front and insisted that young Hill take part. The colonel was impressed. It was the start of the longest professional relationship in Benny's life.

Years later, Bill Day, who was by then a publican, decided that he owed Benny a favour. He booked him as the cabaret at his pub. Benny turned up but the audience didn't. Bill paid him off with a cheque for thirty pounds which Benny put in his pocket. Later still he met Harry Segal, now back in showbusiness proper, in the Charing Cross Road. Harry had been offered a panto booking but couldn't afford the costumes he was required to supply.

How much were they, asked Benny. About thirty pounds, said Harry. Benny pulled Bill Day's still uncashed cheque out of his pocket, took it to a bank, and handed over thirty pounds to a grateful Harry. The favour had come full circle.

Though Benny's original meeting with Richard Stone was to be a watershed in both their lives, starting an association that was to last over forty years, Richard cannot now remember much about it. 'I suppose Benny must have done his comic German act, that thing about the "busten-halter". I just remember thinking he was jolly funny, and saying, "When we're both out of the army, get in touch," or something like that.' Then they forgot all about one another.

After the war Richard Stone became an agent. One day in 1948, he and impresario Hedley Claxton were casting a summer show for the Lido Theatre, Margate. They'd booked Reg Varney to star. Reg, later to have a huge TV success with his own situation comedy *On the Buses*, was then a popular young comic but he needed a straight man.

'Hedley said let's go and look at that Benny Hill fellow out at Kilburn and see if he would do,' said Richard. He would. Reg and Benny often shared a dressing-room, as if on equal billing, and worked out some very funny routines between them, but there was no doubt who was top dog. It was Reg. And he earned the lion's share of the money. Richard Stone was now Benny's agent but still didn't appreciate his new client's potential. Reg Varney was still his big earner and Reg was the one he concentrated on. 'If Benny was getting sixteen pounds a week, Reg must have been getting at least seventy-five. As an agent you concentrate on your highest earner, and when I took people to see the act, I took them to see Reg not Benny.' Richard concedes: 'It would be conceited of me to say that I spotted Benny's tremendous talent because I didn't. I never realized he was going to be a huge star until he started in TV, because the theatre was never his medium.'

Until Richard became his agent, Benny had struggled on alone, but he managed to give the impression that he was a seasoned and successful performer.

Bob Monkhouse met Benny in November 1947 in a show called the *Spotlight Revue* in Notting Hill. Benny had only just changed his name from Alfie, and it was spelt wrongly as 'Bennie' in the programme. To Bob, several years younger, Benny seemed hugely confident, experienced and wise. 'He was the guy who had done it, been on the music halls,' Bob said, 'but he said this was his first professional engagement in the West End. He thought Notting Hill was the West End. I was terrifically impressed by him.'

Benny was rather patronizing to Bob, who says he didn't mind because Benny had not got many people he could be patronizing to. 'He loved being able to say to me, "You'll get your knees brown eventually, my son," and I believed him totally. I listened. I didn't know what I was doing.'

Benny used to phone Bob at his parents' house and tell him about dates he could get. 'Once he told me to go to the Ridgeway Club, Hammersmith, where I would get three big ones. I spent 6s. 8d (34p) going to Victoria station, plus my fare on the underground to Hammersmith, found my way to this club, did my one-liners to a completely indifferent audience, till they got noisy and a man threw a pint of beer over me, went back on stage and did some more and was hit with a small cardboard box of nails which a man threw at me,' said

Bob. 'So I retreated. The boss said, "If Benny Hill recommended you, I don't think I'll be using him again either." I told him I'd been promised three big ones, and he said, "Yes, I stand by my promises," and he gave me three half crowns. So that was what a big one was! I left with 7s 6d having made a net loss on the evening and learned something about Benny's advice.'

But Benny did sometimes make big money. Comparatively speaking, anyway. Another struggling young contemporary, Max Bygraves, was equally generous in recommending his pals for engagements he couldn't do himself. He wrote to one social club apologizing for the fact that he would not be available on the date required but added that he knew a fellow called Benny Hill whom he could get to do it instead. Benny recalled that he got all of £2 10s (£2.50) that night.

Bob Monkhouse watched Benny appear in several shows, and studied his technique. 'He had picked up a lot of German speech while in Germany and he would jam this bowler hat on his head which bent his ears down, and do this very funny voice as Toto the German. He developed this technique for filling in if the audience didn't laugh, by continuing to talk. Having done the punchline, he would look at the ground and continue talking in a low voice, a strange kind of hesitant muttering as if he were communing with himself. Then he'd pick up on the next joke.'

Benny was still terribly insecure, despite the blasé impression he had tried to convey to colleagues like Bob, and sometimes was physically sick when he came off stage. It was about this time Bob began to suspect that Benny's personality on stage was not him at all. 'It was an invention, a confection. A lot of people have done this, they send out the puppet not the puppet master.

Somewhere in the wings remains the real person, unexposed and therefore not vulnerable to rejection.'

Perhaps it was Benny's own vulnerability which made him so sympathetic to fellow professionals. He would never during his life say something unkind about another artist. He and Bob went together once to see a top comedian at the Metropole, Edgware Road, and on the bill was a second comic who just 'died'.

Bob said: 'He was simply awful, his timing was off, his material was dolorous, he looked miserable, he was perfectly dreadful. In those days I – God forgive me – was simply jubilant if someone failed, because it would make me look good by comparison. But Benny was moved to tears. He said, "Oh, that was horrible, that poor fellow." After a few moments, he added thoughtfully, "He had lovely socks." It was the only good thing he could say about him! For years afterwards we called that comic "the man with the socks". And Benny would insist, "He wasn't as bad as all that." '

Bob found Benny a very benevolent fellow with a kindly view of mankind, but there was also something so single-minded about him that it created a barrier between him and the world. 'It would be harsh to say he was selfish, and I'm not saying it in a pejorative sense, but if you take away the pejorative meaning of the word, Benny WAS selfish, totally concerned with himself. He would exercise only his own whims.'

Benny developed a fear of audiences that would later force him to give up live work altogether, but he didn't have the traditional angst of the clown. Simple stage fright would never make him waver from his conviction that one day he would be a top comedian. He had an odd way of coping with self-doubt, according to Bob. The pair of them were sitting in a coffee bar one day with singer

Jean Bayliss, who was quite keen on Benny. They were having an earnest conversation about self-criticism and self-improvement. Jean said you had to be critical of yourself, otherwise you would never improve. Benny said: 'Oh, I've got a trick to get round that.' Jean told him he shouldn't use a trick, he should face up to his problems. But Benny insisted he had a trick. 'As soon as I think I've done anything wrong, I clap my hands and give myself a round of applause. And the feeling goes away.' The other two were nonplussed.

Once he was taken up by Stone and Hedley Claxton, Benny may have worked quite solidly, but he was still not exactly what he could honestly term a success. Richard once booked him into a cine-variety show on Bognor Pier at Christmas. Cine-variety was a strange hybrid where a comic would come on between the films, doing two or three turns a night. In this instance, it was meant to be five times nightly, but business was bad. 'We went down there and there was absolutely no one there,' said Richard. 'The fellow in charge said, "Well if anyone turns up, we'd better do it. Otherwise, don't bother." He didn't even bother to screen the film the last three times.'

Despite such failures, Benny enjoyed the notion of being able to say to people: 'I've got the colonel working for me now,' and the two men were very chummy. Richard and his wife Sara went to Paris for a holiday with Benny, and had a wonderful time going to shows and taking trips down the Seine on the *bateaux mouches*. Benny bought Sara a parasol which she treasured for years.

One year, Sara and Benny found themselves working in the same town. They had a meal together after their respective shows and then shared a taxi home. When they got to Benny's, he invited her in for a nightcap, but she said: 'No, I won't come up.' Benny teased her about it for years afterwards. 'Nice woman that Sara Stone,' he would say, 'but unfortunately she doesn't come up.'

On one memorable occasion the Stones went to Positano in Italy on holiday and invited Benny to join them. When the couple got there, though, they found the place infested by jelly-fish and decided to move on to another resort, forgetting all about the invitation. When Benny arrived at the house in Positano, there was nobody there. 'I'm surprised he didn't leave the agency there and then,' said Richard.

The relationship between the two men was unique in one way: Richard was the only person Benny ever really had rows with. They fought a lot. The Benny Hill famed throughout showbusiness for being so polite and not losing his temper disappeared when he was with his agent.

'It was suggested to me that I had become a substitute father. He had always had a difficult relationship with his father, and he carried on the same sort of thing with me. It was very stormy. When things went wrong, large or small, he blamed me. But often in showbusiness when artists have stormy relationships with people, they walk out. Benny never left. He was still there.'

Their worst row, and the only time Benny ever did threaten to leave the agency, was over a woman. He blamed Stone for introducing him to a girl who didn't want to know. He was sufficiently wounded to lay the whole fiasco at Stone's door and say he wanted another agent. But he changed his mind.

'I think he trusted me. He was a very insecure person, and he was always worried that people were trying to cheat him or take some financial advantage. Ours was a good office to be with. I had the reputation of being straight and honest, and as far as money was concerned, he trusted us totally. He respected my financial advice if not my artistic advice.'

In fact, Richard had long since stopped trying to give Benny any advice about his work. He could see it was neither required nor welcomed. 'When he did live work, my advice was minimal. I might say, "I can't hear you." When I went to the TV shows, I might say I thought a sketch was a bit long, but it stopped there.'

Over the years, the social friendship between the two gradually tailed off. Benny would become far more of a loner anyway as years went by, but he reduced his relationship with his agent to a purely professional one. The Stones were famous for their New Year's Eve parties, but even in the early days, Benny would turn up for half an hour and then leave. Later, he did not go at all. Invitations to join them for Christmas were always politely declined. In 1988, when Richard threw a huge party to celebrate fifty years in showbusiness, Benny was one of the few clients who didn't attend. 'It became a much more "hands off" relationship as the years went on. It was very austere. But that was the way Benny wanted it.'

Until Richard started living part of the year in America, he went to every TV show Benny made. 'I would go down to the studios during the day, watch the run-through, sit through the actual recording in the evening, and go to his dressing-room afterwards to collect him. Then I would carry his plastic bags to the car and drive him home. I was never once invited into the flat for a nightcap, not once. My real function, apart from the financial one, ended up as bag carrier.'

4

A Television Star is Born

Despite being singled out for a favourable mention by the
Daily Telegraph's distinguished reviewer W.A. Darlington
when he appeared in a 1948 revue at the Boltons Theatre,
South Kensington, Benny always knew in his heart that
live theatre work as not his forte. As the singer Shani
Wallis observed once: 'Benny is a hit for the first five
rows.' He didn't project himself much further, Bob Monkhouse agreed, nor did he seem very interested in doing
so, even though he had the necessary vocal power. Bob
said: 'Big audiences embarrassed him. He was quite
clearly inhibited by the presence of a large number of
people. I believe he performed in front of a mirror when
he started. The result was an inhibited performance
which he had to inflate and inflate to get as far as Row J.'
And he was at his worst when he had to appear as himself
doing a string of patter jokes, or acting as compère.
He was far, far better when he came on as one of his
characters like the German.

He hated it if someone he knew was in the audience. It
inhibited him even further. If members of his proud
family sat in the audience, it upset him. 'He didn't mind
if you turned up in the audience without telling him and
then went round after to see him,' said Chris Hill. 'But he
didn't like to know you were there to begin with. He used

to have terrible rows with his dad about it, because his father always made a big performance about going to go to his shows. "I'm this, I'm the other, I'm Benny Hill's father." Typical Uncle Alf. Benny used to go absolutely wild about it. So I learned to creep in quietly without Benny seeing me.'

He was straight man to Reg Varney for two or three years, but was sometimes allowed to do his own little turn as well. It was not exactly the big time. At one point, he and Reg wanted to do a new boxing sketch in a show booked by the impresarios George and Alfred Black. The Blacks were not too keen on the idea, so Richard Stone suggested that the sketch was tried out in some other show where the Blacks could come and see it. It needed five people altogether, so Stone recruited Ian Carmichael, Ian Wallace and Philip Dale. He booked the sketch at Poplar Town Hall for the grand sum of fifty pounds. 'I paid them each ten pounds, which they were glad of at the time, and then the cheque I got from the agent at Poplar bounced, so they all owed me a tenner.'

Still frustrated at being a mere straight man and determined to make it in his own right, Benny now persuaded the Blacks to let him do his own regular solo spot in the show as well as acting as Reg's 'feed' and as company manager. But he died the death. When he got to Newcastle and Sunderland there were so many bad reports that the Blacks insisted the solo turn had to go. One night Benny got the slow handclap and Reg Varney wept in sympathy as Benny came off stage and threw up. The Blacks decreed that in future he could keep the same money but just work with Reg and as company manager. Benny said no. Richard Stone, who is the first to admit he still didn't see which direction Benny should take, tried to make him change his mind. But Benny was adamant and left the show.

He had a tough time over the next few months but he had realized where his future lay when he saw a television for the first time in a shop window.

He started sending sketches to Ronnie Waldman, entertainment supremo in the burgeoning BBC TV service. In August 1951, he was rewarded with his first television appearance on a show called 'Hi There!' The budget for the whole programme was £400. Next morning, the *News Chronicle* said: 'If neither his material nor his background was brilliant, Benny demonstrated that with the help of an experienced TV scriptwriter he could be one of the brightest comics on TV.' They were wrong there. Apart from a successful collaboration with Dave Freeman in his BBC days, Benny wrote all his best material himself.

Nevertheless it was enough to get him a second booking, in a show called 'Starlight Symphony' screened live, ironically, from the 1951 'Radio Show'. Critic Leonard Mosley bemoaned the lack of a really big name in the show, but acknowledged that the unknown young man who acted as comperè-comedian 'has charm and manner and can get his tongue round some amusing dialect stories and songs'. Slipping the knife in, he added: 'The only trouble being that people like Jon Pertwee do the same thing rather better.' But more perceptive people inside the BBC had realized that Benny was a natural TV performer. A few months later, he was booked as regular presenter of a monthly talent-spotting show called 'The Centre Show', which came from a forces' canteen called the Nuffield Centre.

Among those who saw his début was a schoolboy called Tony Warren, who a decade later would create 'Coronation Street'. Benny came on as a yeoman and sang one of his ballads. Tony said: 'I have never been more certain that I was watching a big TV star in the making, he stood out head and shoulders above the rest. He was a TV natural. Apart from being funny, he had tremendous charm. The whole thing was like a trailer for stardom.'

A year later, Benny upset the War Office with one of his jokes, a line about someone losing their football coupon. The punchline was a play on the phone number of Scotland Yard – Whitehall 1212 – and the way football results were scored on the coupon with one point for a home win and two for an away win: Whitehall Home Away, Home Away. Some colonel thought he'd heard Benny refer to Whitehall as 'Homo Way'. So the War Office asked the BBC to submit all scripts for the show for official vetting in advance. The BBC backed Benny. They changed the name of the series to 'The Services Show', and mounted it at the TV studios instead of the Nuffield Centre, so that it no longer had any War Office connection.

In 1953, according to Richard Stone, Benny was averaging about twenty pounds a week, and spent a lot of time out of work. But it gave him the opportunity to write more and more material for his new medium. And in 1954, the BBC announced he would be given his own 'Benny Hill Show' starting in January 1955. They had recognized, as he had, that he understood television like few other performers.

As soon as he saw it, he realized the possibilities of the close-up. He recognized that the merest twitch of the corner of his mouth or the conspiratorial gleam in his eye could be conveyed to every member of the home audience, not just to the first two rows of the stalls. Looking into the camera was as painless as looking into the mirror he had practised on. But if he had any real insights into the way his technique worked, he never divulged them. He would just say that he'd spent his early years watching Buster Keaton, Charlie Chaplin and the rest, and something must have rubbed off.

Now the characters he invented like Fred Scuttle took over from the diffident Benny Hill. Bob Monkhouse said: 'He didn't so much hide behind a character as invade it. He would invent a character which was really rather paper thin, and then invest it with so much energy and so much sly charm, that you would think if you didn't join in the joke you were missing something. He was continually implying, rather like Arthur Askey, that this whole thing was ridiculous but let's do it together. And it was enormously effective. Audiences loved him on TV where he came through the glass of the tube and seemed to be in the room with them. He found the technique of inflating his performance just exactly to the point where he penetrated the camera and the TV screen. He became a Midas who could turn trashy material from dull lead into sparkling gold.'

Very soon Benny was a household name. I remember a boy at school called Paul Hill who was immediately re-christened Benny in honour of our new hero, and remained Benny Hill for the remainder of his schooldays.

Schoolgirl Bella Emberg, later to appear in many editions of 'The Benny Hill Show' herself, was also a fan. Her family had no TV yet, so she used to see his shows at the home of her friend Lola Baker. When Benny appeared at the Brighton Hippodrome, the two girls not only went to see the show, but decided to wait for him at the stagedoor afterwards. 'I suppose we thought we'd be the only ones, but about a thousand others had the same idea. I've never seen that stagedoor so jam-packed with people.'

Years later, Benny told Bella that he could pack the country's theatres for a year on the strength of one TV show, such was the power of TV in those early novelty years. But it didn't make him enjoy live work any better.

By 1958, his Saturday BBC show was getting twelve million viewers. Considering that television had not reached complete saturation point by then, and that ITV was hitting back with some strong weekend entertainment, this is a considerable achievement. The BBC's annual report in October that year named Benny as its most popular artist, with a third of the population regularly watching his shows. That year, he also made a special for Lew Grade's ATV, but returned to the BBC afterwards.

He made several films during this period, but like so many other comics, found that the intimacy of his approach, which worked so well in the living-room, did not translate successfully to the big screen. He also had the problem of not being in total control and seeing what he often thought was his best work end up on the cutting-room floor.

His films included *Who Done It?*, a comedy thriller created especially for him and built around his central character. But as with many other TV comedians, including Morecambe and Wise, the format of a feature-length film proved not to be the ideal vehicle for his humour. He plays smaller character parts in *Chitty Chitty Bang Bang*, *The Italian Job* and *Those Magnificent Men in Their Flying Machines*. *The Italian Job* served to enrol co-star Michael Caine as a life-long member of Benny's fan club. But much as he laughed at and admired Benny, Michael later admitted that at the end of all the weeks they worked together, he knew as little about the man as when they started. Benny also co-starred with Tommy Steele in *Light*

Up the Sky, but alas, none of his screen performances really did light up the sky. He dreamed of writing, directing and starring in his own film, and when he switched to ITV in 1968, one of the plans was for him to do just that. In the event, he made two silent movies, *The Waiters* and *Eddie in August.* But he never made any real impact as a cinema star.

He also did the almost obligatory stint as tutor to radio's dummy schoolboy, Archie Andrews. Radio hardly seemed the best career move for a comedian whose face would be his fortune, but it had been a stepping stone for many other rising comics, and since he was working with a ventriloquist whose audience could not see whether he moved his lips or not, it was strangely appropriate.

Benny dreamed of being an impresario. He had always been a great spotter of talent, and would pack his TV shows with musical numbers from artists he had found on his travels. He was besotted with South American music, not only introducing Los Trios Paraguayos to British TV, but trying to learn how to play the South American instruments himself.

As he told Bella Emberg, his TV fame boosted his theatre appearances to the point where he could really name his own price. Typically, he balanced the amount of money he could earn against the agony his live appearances caused him and decided to cut them out. He did not need the money. Always his own man, he was probably unique in British showbusiness in confining himself to television from then on. He gave up summer seasons and West End revues without a moment's regret. His last appearance on a stage, apart from a couple of charity shows, was at Sydney Town Hall in 1960.

He told me: 'I think you should do what you're good at. I figure I understand television, and I don't understand the stage. I was eighteen months at the Prince of Wales in the Folies Bergères show, with Tommy Cooper and lots of nice ladies, and six or eight months at the Palace with Shani Wallis and Robertson Hare and Irving Davies and his dancers. That's a lot of shows, and I was never comfortable. I was never the sort who liked turning out on a November night when it's raining and you've got to go and do two houses. Especially on a Friday. The first is going to be empty and the second maybe quite full. But you never know when there's going to be drunks in, and you can't cut and do it again if they spoil it, like you can in TV.'

Benny's grumbles didn't end with the performance. He went on: 'Then I'd come out backstage in Soho and there'd be half a dozen nice people saying, "Can I have your autograph?" and a dozen football hooligans throwing things at me. And a lot worse than that can happen too! So why do it? And doing the same thing night after night, too.'

He claimed that in the Prince of Wales show, he was so tired and bored he'd often sing the same verse of one of his madrigals twice. 'When I was making films as well, I was having a very heavy time. I was so tired I didn't know what I was doing. When I made *Who Done It?* I'd be going off to the studio at 5.30 or 6 in the morning, having come off stage at 11 p.m. I'd have taken off my make-up, said goodnight to everyone backstage, signed a few autographs, gone home, had a bath and then set the alarm for 5.30 a.m., and I'd be lucky if I got to bed by 2 or 3. I remember in one film scene where I had to lie on the floor, I fell fast asleep! I used to fall asleep in the make-up chair, wake up and look at the mirror and see a totally different person with hair and warts everywhere. I suddenly thought to myself, "At this rate I'm going to be the richest man in the cemetery." Who wants that? I certainly don't.'

The greatest relief in cutting down on work was that it enabled him to leave the horrors of a huge theatre audience behind. The pattern he eventually developed for the TV shows was to film as much as possible on location, and then spend several days in the studio doing the complicated sketches such as the split-screen effects he loved, like the pioneering programme in which he played all the panellists on 'Juke Box Jury'. Then he would spend one evening in the studio with the audience. Even there, he liked the crowd to be as small as was possible for the amount of laughter and applause that was required of them. They would be shown all the pre-recorded sketches so that their responses could be captured on sound, and Benny would make as brief an appearance as possible live in front of them. Even that filled him with terror.

5

Lifestyle

For several years Benny lived in an unimposing flat in Edgware Road, reputed to boast only cold water, but in 1960 he moved to a splendid address befitting a top TV star. No. 2 Queensgate was a corner flat with huge windows and a balcony looking across the road to Hyde Park. Below was the equine statue at the top of the wide sweep of Queensgate.

His lifestyle never quite lived up to his address, though. Basically it was terribly self-indulgent, inasmuch as he pleased himself totally without worrying what other people thought. Unencumbered by the demands of a family or a nine-to-five job, he gave in to his every whim.

It seemed eccentric, simply because it did not often involve spending much of the money he earned. His indifference to money was part of his charm. His idiosyncracies were otherwise unremarkable. If he wanted to stay in for days without seeing anyone, he did. If he wanted to go wandering off around Europe without any luggage, he did. If he wanted to wear cheap clothes, he did. If he wanted to listen to records of Latin-American music for hours, he did. He loved French music too, and would don a beret and smoke a cheroot while he listened to it. Even when Benny became a multi-millionaire, Richard Stone thought his records were probably the most valuable things he possessed. He owned little else. Ownership was too much trouble. His tastes were simple. He liked travelling, he liked food, he liked girls and he liked work. He enjoyed the cinema and some spectator sports, especially boxing, but literature and politics largely passed him by. Every book he ever read was about show-business. He saw the ways of the world only in terms of the comedy they produced.

He was totally unembarrassed about the fact that he spent every Christmas watching television. He couldn't understand how other people found time to do anything else. The greatest invention of the last fifty years, in his opinion, was the video recorder which allowed him to double, if not triple his viewing. The TV set was the focal point of every room he occupied. Television was his obsession.

His restless travelling began with a fondness for the less fashionable parts of France and Spain. Later, he progressed to the Côte d'Azur. Then he started going to the Far East on his way to see his sister Diana who now lived in Australia. She had gone out there to work as a nurse, married and settled down to raise a family. Benny later arranged for his parents to spend six months out there with her, but when he went himself, his trip would often be financed by a TV company who had invited him to do a show, or an advertising agency who wanted him to make a commercial. Why pay himself if someone else was willing to do so? But his favourite type of travel was the impromptu unplanned holiday. He used to ring up the West London air terminal, then situated a few hundred yards from his flat, ask them where the next available flight was going and book a seat. He travelled without any luggage, buying clean shirts and underwear as he needed them. He would sometimes travel in luxury, sometimes he would rough it. It depended how the fancy took him. He loved the Camargue, the marshy delta in France where the white horses roam, and would walk for miles there. He adored the rather seedy areas of Marseilles. But he also liked staying at the Georges V in Paris and dining at Maxim's. None of his habits was dictated by cost, whatever people said, but purely by whim. He did what he wanted to do and went where he wanted to go. He coded his favourite European cities by how many days he could stay there without getting bored. Nice was an eight-day city, because he could go to Cannes and Juan Les Pins and Monte Carlo while he was there. Others were shorter. He plied his friends back home with postcards, signed Little Ben or Wee Ben, or if he was in France, Petit Ben. Or even That Nice Benny Hill.

When he was younger, Benny was a notable cook and was fond of inviting people to dinner parties at Queensgate, going to enormous trouble to prepare elaborate dishes. He loved taking people out for meals as well, and would travel a long way to a good restaurant. But later he discovered the equal delights of Marks and Spencer's recipe meals. He would walk across Hyde Park to Marks and Spencer's in Oxford Street, do his shopping, and walk back. Halfway he would sit on a park bench, and scoff any item in his shopping that didn't need cooking. He always chose a seat that faced away from the footpath so that people wouldn't spot him. Sometimes they did, sometimes they mistook him for a tramp, eating out of a carrier bag.

For many years there were rumours that Benny was gay, based one can only suppose, on the fact that he never married. Certainly the people who started these rumours cannot have known him. He was so overtly heterosexual in his tastes and conversation, it perplexed him that anyone could mistake his inclinations. Perhaps they thought he protested too much, since he talked about girls constantly. No woman could be with him for more than a few minutes and still harbour any illusion that he might be gay. He adored women and he showed it. Not in any offensive way, simply by sparkling in their company, by being gallant and attentive. He was an old-fashioned ladies' man.

Benny was very attractive when he was young. 'He was comparatively slender, a good height, he had that thick corn-silk-coloured hair, and a lovely humorous, steady gaze,' said Bob Monkhouse. 'Girls turned on to him very quickly. He certainly did like the girls and plenty of them.'

The younger and the less sophisticated they were the more secure he felt. He used to say that he would like to marry a girl from a very poor background, whom he could rescue and introduce to a life without worry, like a knight on a white charger. He often claimed that his favourite girls were simple, working-class girls whom he could impress by offering them treats. Perhaps he didn't have any faith in his ability to impress them with his personality. He was plagued with shyness, which made him impatient of the niceties of the courting ritual. His favourite method of meeting women, according to Bob, was to hang around the dance halls of Hammersmith and Tottenham Court Road, nursing an orange squash until someone recognized the famous face and came to talk to him, thus saving him the agonies of having to make the first approach. 'Then he would take them to the Cocoa House in Regent Street and buy them a cocoa. But among women of any sophistication and strength of opinion he felt completely out of his depth and would leave.'

Benny actually dated Jackie Monkhouse, then Bob's

secretary and now his second wife, a couple of times. He took her to a party at Bob's house. 'She found him tremendously charming, but as soon as she sort of express-ed herself in any affirmative way, he shrank away,' said Bob. 'And he was clearly overwhelmed by the people who were there on this occasion, Harold Pinter and Denis Norden and their wives. Benny hadn't got much tolerance for alcohol then. He had a couple of drinks within the first twenty minutes and was clearly inebriated. He excused himself to go outside and clear his head and never came back!'

Benny's great friend was Peter Charlesworth, orig-inally a song plugger and eventually a successful show-business agent. They laughed together, went on holiday together, chased girls together. What Benny lacked in confidence, Peter made up for in chat.

Benny was tremendously loyal to his friends from this era, like his old Army pal Harry Segal and scriptwriter Dave Freeman. If one of them was short of cash, Benny would pay over the odds for an idea for a gag, as a tactful way of helping them out. He did this with Charlesworth. In fact, his loyalty to him was so great that when Peter became an agent, Richard Stone anticipated that Benny would leave him to join Charlesworth's agency. 'After all, he was not just a very close friend, he was a supplier of crumpet. And I could never be that, because I was already married when I first knew him. I was surprised that Benny stayed with me, but he did.'

When the flat next door to his became vacant, Benny had the two knocked into one and his home became even more imposing. In theory anyway. The interior could hardly be called impressive. He just never bothered to do anything about it. Interior design didn't interest him, he thought good taste was something to do with food. He

had plain cream walls, dull curtains, few pictures or personal knick-knacks. To add a bit of colour, he would buy
all the most colourful liqueurs, such as Punt e Mes and
Parfait Amour, and range the bottles on the sideboard. 'I
used to go into Peter Dominic's, and buy them purely by
the look of the bottle. You've never seen so much booze,'
he told me. When his weight became a problem, he
stopped doing it because it put too much temptation in
his way.

His most treasured possessions were his TV set and a
huge bow-fronted walnut radiogram, plus a few things
he later brought up from his mother's home including a
favourite table lamp. Otherwise, the furniture was sparse,
and looked as if it had come from the fifties' equivalent
of MFI, according to actor Jon Jon Keefe who went back
there after an evening's night-clubbing. 'We had champagne and all the bits and pieces which was what you
expected from a star,' he said, 'but the rest of it wasn't.
The radiogram looked like the one my dad had bought
just after the war, and there was a picture of Benny with
the Queen at a Royal Variety Show which was all tinged
with age and curling up out of the frame. He just didn't
care a fig about money or about what people thought of
him. He lived exactly as he wanted.'

In the late seventies, the magazine *TV Times* asked
Benny if he would take part in one of their regular features
in which they redesigned and furnished part of a star's
home and then photographed the result. Benny agreed.
His decision had less to do with the fact that they were
going to pay for it, more with the thought that it would
save him the trouble. It hurt him when people criticized
his living conditions and he thought this would deflect
the sneers.

TV Times set about turning his huge living-room into a

setting suitable for a sophisticated bachelor star. It was not a success. 'Beforehand, it was functional and rather mundane, but quite cosy. It was him,' said actress Jenny Lee-Wright. 'Afterwards the place looked like a cardboard cut-out.' The magazine decided to make it look as if Benny was throwing a party for other stars for the picture session, and told him whom they planned to invite. He was indignant. He didn't know any of them. He said: 'I'll have my girls from the show at the party or nobody.'

He invited Louise English, one of his special favourites: 'You won't let me down, will you? You will turn up?' She said: 'I knew when I arrived it was all a disaster. Benny opened the door still wearing his carpet slippers and looking very unhappy. The room was ghastly. There was navy blue carpet all up the walls, spotlights everywhere and these huge pale velvet chesterfields. There were bowls of flowers and little homely touches. But once the photos had been taken, they cleared all the homely touches away. They were just props! Without them it looked cold and unwelcoming.'

When all the magazine people had gone, Benny shut the door firmly on the living-room and led Louise to another room in the flat. 'Look at this,' he said. Inside were all the bits and pieces that used to be in the living-room, including his mother's table lamp. He'd just re-created it in another room. From then on, he lived in the smaller room and only used the smart one for entertaining and for people he wanted to impress. I was taken out of what became known as the 'carpet room' and into the cosy room on my third visit. I felt very honoured.

Benny spent twenty-five years in the flat, virtually all the time on his own. Though he loved entertaining and talked about his visitors in a way that implied he had people there constantly, they were actually quite rare. He rattled round in the place like a plump pea in a rather elegant can, perfectly happy with his own company. He was a loner, but not lonely. His life only seemed sad to outsiders, to him it was not tragic in any way. Because of an inability to relate to normal mundane preoccupations, he did not know what he was missing. Work occupied the major part of his thoughts at all times. Even his holidays were opportunities to sit and observe people in the hope that something they did or said might give him an idea for a sketch.

His contact with the people he worked with was kept to a minimum outside the TV studios, especially the men. He would ring up long-time associate Bob Todd and tell him he'd just been to Spain and he'd seen someone who sent his regards. 'And that would be about it,' said Bob. 'Conversation was difficult with Benny. I got the impression he sometimes felt like having someone to talk to, but then couldn't think of anything to say.'

Benny was happy, though. On his fiftieth birthday, he told a long-time colleague Henry McGee, rather to Henry's surprise: 'I've had a very happy life, I've done everything I ever wanted. I wouldn't mind if I went tomorrow.'

He was still close to his parents who were terribly proud of his success. They would come up to London and he'd take them to a show and afterwards for a meal. In the summer of 1971, he took his father on holiday to Spain. He confessed that he felt quite nervous about it because he thought the Captain would try to take control of the whole thing as usual, even though it was Benny who really knew Spain well. But the Captain had mellowed. The holiday was a great success and Benny was so pleased that he'd done it, because his father died on 6 May the following year. His mother survived to her eighties, but was crippled with arthritis for the last few years, and lived in a nursing home. Early in 1976 she asked if she could go home to Westrow Gardens for a while and it was there, nursed with tender loving care by her precious son, that she died on 10 February. As he was to admit on 'Omnibus' years later, Benny did not show his grief. He was composed at the funeral, standing with Aunt Louie. His mother had made him promise never to sell Westrow Gardens and he honoured the promise. He was more openly upset when Diana died of cancer in 1984. The end came quickly, and he did not even have time to visit her, which upset him terribly.

Unfortunately relations with his brother had deteriorated. Their schoolboy fights turned into a rather prickly relationship in adulthood. About twenty years ago, they fell out and did not speak for years. Over what, no one really knew. They even disagreed about the cause of the split. Leonard would sometimes tell people it was because Benny had sided with their mother in some row over Leonard's wedding plans. Other times he claimed they had just drifted apart. Benny's version was that it had all been about money. There had been some stupid misunderstanding, and before it could be sorted out, Leonard had come charging up to London from his home in Sussex. There had been a scene at the door of the flat in Queensgate. Dignity had been ruffled, feelings hurt on both sides.

Chris Hill says he never knew what it was about, but he made various efforts over the years to try to bring the pair together. Sometimes he just tactfully suggested to Benny that it was time they patched things up. Once he took matters into his own hands and deliberately put the two men into the same car at a family funeral. They spoke on that occasion, but it did not heal the breach.

Star of his own BBC show in 1955, Benny is still living modestly in Kilburn (*Associated Press*).

In 1959, Benny returned for a day to his old job for the benefit of the local press (*Southern Evening Echo*).

Benny with the girl he loved, Annette André, in the Blue Angel, in 1963 (*Annette André*).

The brothers reached some sort of truce in the late eighties, but Benny was still uneasy about the relationship. Leonard took to coming to Thames' studios in 1988 to research a book, and Benny's eyes would roll resignedly every time his portly brother lumbered into view. But when Leonard died in 1990, things had been repaired sufficiently for Benny to attend the funeral.

6

Love

Until he was about forty, Benny fell in love regularly and deeply. Emotionally immature, he seemed not to be able to discuss his feelings with the women concerned, or to gauge whether a relationship had reached the point where talk of marriage would be welcomed. Proposals were always on the tip of his tongue. He was rumoured to have proposed to film star Belinda Lee during the making of his first film, *Who Done It?* After knowing her for only two weeks, he invited her to a meal in the studio commissary, and asked her to marry him.

It was as if, said one acquaintance, there were no gradations between meeting a woman, falling for her and being her husband. His approach was so jejune as to be meaningless, and any girl relatively well-versed in the ways of the world would have thought he was crazy. After saying everything he had to say to a girl, he had nothing left to offer but, 'Will you marry me then?'

One of his early passions was for a beautiful young actress called Elaine, who was later to marry an international star. She was also a client of Richard Stone's agency and Benny met her when Richard booked them both on to the same radio show. 'He was madly in love with her,' said Stone. 'Madly. I am absolutely certain of that.' But she didn't want to know. The lovelorn comic used to follow her around London until he was forced to admit defeat. Then he blamed Richard Stone for the whole fiasco. They had one of their worst ever rows, the one occasion on which Benny threatened to leave the agency. His anger and pain were somehow transferred to the man who had introduced him to the girl who had then snubbed him.

Chris Hill met one of Benny's girls when he was visiting him in London in the fifties, and had the impression that this one was the great love of his cousin's life. She was a dancer, pretty and very tiny. But the relationship soon broke up. 'I believe she went off and married someone else, an Arab,' said Chris. 'Benny did not seem to want to talk about it afterwards, so I never liked to raise the subject.'

Benny made serious proposals to several women. One at least must have accepted him. For a while in the 1950s, he considered himself engaged to a girl who worked as an air hostess. But though she was very fond of him, it fizzled out. And he rarely mentioned it afterwards. Sometimes he asked women to marry him without them even realizing that he was in love with them in the first place. None of the women involved appears really to have loved him in return.

In later life, he was asked over and over why he had never married, and he had his usual rehearsed answers to the inquiries, as he did to any question which tried to get under his skin. Sometimes he just made silly jokes like: 'Why buy a book when you can join a library?' Or: 'Why burn the house down just because you want some toast?' Or he'd say: 'Well, you see, I do a lot of flying and I like a window seat.'

If he decided to elaborate, however, his most frequent story was that the two great loves of his life had both been actresses. He said he had proposed to the first from a phone box because he didn't have the courage to ask her to her face. She told him she needed time to think about it, but then said no, and later married a Harley Street dentist. He had also proposed to the second one who had turned him down and broken his heart so badly that he had decided never to allow himself to be hurt again. He had avoided deep emotional attachments from then on and that was why he had never wed.

The story varied slightly each time he told it. Sometimes he said it was one dancer and one actress, or two dancers. Sometimes it was the rejected proposal from the phone box which had done the real emotional damage. Sometimes it was the later relationship which had made him determined never to risk being rejected again. I often wondered if any of it were true, or if it was all just something he made up to explain to the curious why he remained a bachelor. After all, it was a nice line – the broken heart and the determination never to be hurt again. It gained him instant sympathy and put paid to further questions.

When I asked him, he told me the real heartbreaker had been the second actress. He described how she had subsequently appeared in a commercial which would be on ITV several times in an evening. While he could avoid the television drama in which she appeared, he never knew when the advert was going to be on. So it caught him unawares each time, and seeing her positively tormented him. He would say that he sometimes had to leave the room rather than look at the screen. (Being Benny, he couldn't actually switch the television off, of course.) He never told me her name.

At the time, the rumours that he was gay were rife, and one TV industry stalwart who should have known better assured me quite categorically that the mystery 'woman' was actually a male model. It was this man, he insisted, who kept popping up in ITV commercials and ruining Benny's evenings. Absolute nonsense. To several very close friends over the years, he confided the name of his lost love. It was actress Annette André.

Maybe to his male pals he improved the story by claiming they'd had a physical affair. It would have fitted in with the macho image he liked to create. Or maybe he left it all to innuendo and their imagination, and they just jumped to their own conclusions. Certainly his brother Leonard believed it had been a genuinely passionate relationship. 'Benny became besotted with her,' he claimed in *Saucy Boy*, 'but their affair was too intense to last. When his shapely girlfriend began touring in a play, there were fewer opportunities for them to meet. Despite strenuous efforts, Benny was forced to accept defeat.'

The real truth is very different. Annette André was one of the more decorative figures of 'swinging sixties' London. As famous for her social life as for her acting roles, she lived near the Kings Road, the archetypal Chelsea bird with lint-white hair, eyes sooty with make-up, tiny mini-skirts and white Courrèges boots. She is still a beautiful woman now, but in those days she was absolutely stunning.

Benny met her long before she became famous in Britain. Annette began her career as a ballet dancer in her native Australia, but then branched out into acting on radio and television. By her teens she was an all-rounder in the comparatively small world of Australian show-business, presenting a teenage show for a while, acting in straight drama and 'feeding' various comedians.

Benny had already made several shows for the new Australian TV service by this time, and was a popular star. When he returned to do another show it was inevitable they would meet. Annette said: 'I happened to be doing quite a lot of work for the same channel. I used to be the "straight" girl both for Australian comics and for any visiting artists like Benny, so I met him when I was booked for his show. I liked him and he liked me, and I started showing him round Sydney a little.'

In fact, Benny already knew Sydney pretty well, but he did not let this interfere with his dates with the gorgeous blonde. As usual with women in showbusiness, he talked to her about her career. 'I was young and terribly naïve,' she said, 'but he was absolutely sweet. He would always pick me up at the flat where I was living then, and deliver me back there at the end of the evening.' Her mother vaguely recalls meeting Benny when he used to pick Annette up, and thinking that he was very nice, but Benny did not introduce Annette to his own relatives in Australia, sister Diana and her family.

Benny was already a high earner both from his TV shows and the frequent commercials he used to make in those days. But as always, he was touchingly unassuming. 'He never talked about money, he was just so normal and nice, you would never have known he was famous. We'd either go out in a taxi, or we'd walk a lot. Very casual evenings. Sometimes we'd go and buy a lobster and then he'd cook it at the flat he'd rented overlooking the sea. He was a very good cook. I remember him playing Spanish music a lot, he absolutely loved it.'

The relationship remained purely a friendship and never became a romance. 'We were great friends and we had lots of laughs. Somehow or other I just always felt easy with him, and he obviously felt easy with me. He wasn't trying to be funny all the time, that wasn't his style.' It was only later that she realized that when Benny did put on a funny act, it was often to hide his real feelings. When he left Australia, he gave Annette his address and asked her to keep in touch. They wrote occasionally.

The Australian showbusiness scene was not expanding fast enough to accommodate all the native talent, so like many others of her generation, Annette decided to come to Europe. She went to Italy first, arriving there with the grand sum of ten pounds in her pocket, but she survived. Then she landed a small part in a British musical version of *Vanity Fair*, which got her to London. 'The only thing that really bothered me in the beginning was the weather,' she remembered. 'It was the winter of 1962–3, and it knocked me sideways. I ended up getting pneumonia. Then in about April, the sun came out and everything changed.' She shared a Chelsea flat with two granddaughters of Dame Sybil Thorndike, and launched herself on London.

She had already let Benny know that she was coming over. He was an important contact. 'I wanted to get to know as many people as possible,' she admitted. He immediately arranged for her to have some work in a couple of his BBC shows. Her main memory is of dressing up as a gorilla for one sketch.

She went to Benny's flat in Queensgate many times. 'It was very spacious, very sparsely furnished and all the walls seemed to be cream. I was surprised when I saw it for the first time, because it was so simple. I knew he had a lot of money so I expected it to be more elaborate, but he obviously had no talent at all as a homemaker.'

They continued to go out on dates. One of Benny's favourite evenings was going to see the 'Spanish' dancers Dorita e Pepe, who were actually British. The couple were starring in cabaret in a popular Spanish restaurant. Annette shared Benny's love of all things Spanish. 'As an

Australian, you dream of many faraway places, that you only see on postcards and Spain always had a special attraction for me. I just loved the flamenco dancing, Benny and I would clap along with the music and afterwards Dorita and Pepe would come and join us at the table.' A photograph taken of the foursome on one of these evenings shows Annette wearing Pepe's sombrero.

They went to other nightspots too, including one of Benny's favourites called the Blue Angel. But the relationship never progressed beyond a cosy companionship and shared laughter. 'He was an extremely nice man who was very kind to me and got me some work. We used to laugh together and were good friends, but that was it,' Annette told me. 'I didn't have to put on an act for him, I didn't have to fight for my life with him. He was fond of me and I was fond of him and it was cosy.'

Naturally Annette was going out with other men at the time. If Benny had other girlfriends, he never mentioned it. 'He might talk about somebody and say, "Oh, isn't she lovely, isn't she beautiful", but never talked about any relationships.' She and Benny would kiss and cuddle, but nothing more. Benny was good-looking in those days, if overweight, but Annette was never attracted to him sexually. 'I never had an affair with him. I didn't want to, and he was far too sensitive to try to force anyone.' He would tell her about his trips to France and Spain and once suggested she accompanied him next time he went to France. 'But I was working, or something, or else I just shied away from it because I just did not want to have an affair with him,' she said. 'He kind of knew I didn't want to go away with him. He was just so afraid of being hurt or rebuffed, he didn't pursue it.'

The actual proposal of marriage, when it came, was such a shock that Annette can barely recall the circumstances. She thinks it was probably at his Queensgate flat. 'I certainly remember the proposal itself, because it was very significant, but not the actual words he used. I was shocked when he said it. I said something about not being ready for marriage, and not even wanting to think about it at that point in my life. He immediately tried to cover the whole thing up by turning it into a joke and said, "Oh well, who'd want to marry a silly old fat man like me, anyway?" I can see his face sitting across from me as he said it. He didn't look hurt exactly, because Benny never did unless he wanted to look hurt. He was very good at hiding his feelings. But I was embarrassed because this dear friend had suddenly become serious. I wasn't very deep in those days, quite the opposite. I would never have hurt someone deliberately, but I probably hurt quite a few people unintentionally because I was just so young.'

The friendship continued for a while till Annette seized a chance to discover Spain for herself, and accepted an offer to make a film there. While she was in Spain, she met someone with whom she fell deeply in love, the bullfighter known as El Cordobés. When filming finished she decided to stay on. 'I phoned Benny up for a chat from Spain, and he said, "Oh well, when you do come back you must come and see me." But I didn't get in touch.' Her relationship with El Cordobés earned her a lot of newspaper coverage and Benny would undoubtedly have read about it. 'And I suppose I felt bad about it,' she said. 'There was no reason why I should feel bad really, but I never contacted Benny again. It wasn't for him to make the move, because I suppose by then I had really disappointed him. It was up to me, but somehow I didn't.' Without being able to explain why, Annette knew that their friendship was fatally damaged.

She later went on to star in the ITV series 'Randall and Hopkirk Deceased', and did indeed appear in a commercial a few years afterwards. It was for Matchsticks, a kind of after-dinner mint chocolate, and she was seen at her most glamorous, in a late-night, romantic setting, nibbling away at her Matchsticks. It must have cut Benny to the quick.

Annette never told anyone about the proposal except for one close girlfriend, and more recently, her husband, American producer Arthur Weingarten, whom she married in 1989. She did not finally realize the depth of Benny's feelings until his illness in February 1992. A journalist phoned her to tell her Benny was ill in hospital, and asked her how she felt, since she was the one person Benny had really loved and wanted to marry. 'It was a terrible shock. I was shattered. So I phoned him at the Brompton Hospital.'

After nearly thirty years of not speaking to her, the call must have been even more of a shock for Benny. She half expected that he wouldn't even have her put through. But he did. He was surprised to hear from her, but sounded far better than she expected. Annette tried to explain to him that someone had told her 'some things that I'm quite surprised about', and reassured him that she was not going to talk to the press. She found it too painful to elaborate.

Then the conversation moved on to more general things. She told him proudly about her thirteen-year-old daughter, whose father she has never publicly identified, and about her recent marriage. He prattled on about how Michael Jackson had just been to visit him and how they were going to work together when Benny was better. He repeatedly mentioned how badly he wanted to get back to work.

After about fifteen minutes, she suggested that when he was well again, they should meet up, for a drink or a coffee. 'I told him I would love him to meet my husband. I said, "He's very nice and I think you'll like him." ' Benny became very flustered and evasive. 'He said, "We'll see, we'll see, you know I don't see many people these days. I've just got a few friends." And I suddenly thought, "Oh dear, what have I done?" '

She was still disquieted by the whole incident when she heard Benny had died.

7

Sex

Benny decided love was too painful. It hurt too much when it went wrong, and in his case it usually did. So he made a deliberate decision, as far as one can decide about something as unpredictable as love – not to let himself ever fall for anyone again. His sister Diana used to tell him that if he never married, he would have no one to cry at his funeral, and he would say that it was OK by him, because he didn't want anyone to cry for him.

Instead he established the image of himself as the great Lothario practically fighting off girls. He polished it till it dazzled, and deflected people's eyes from the real truth: that he spent most of his time alone. Richard Stone said: 'Every time I went to his flat, he would talk about the girl who had been there the day before and the one who was going to be there tomorrow, but there was never anyone there when I called. Never so much as a sign of a girl. Not once. It was always yesterday and tomorrow.'

If Benny was unsuccessful at love, it is doubtful if he was much more successful at sex. His fear of rejection stopped him from trying very hard. His sexual liaisons, such as they were, were transitory and insignificant. In all the years of his fame, only one girl went to a newspaper and told of an 'affair' with Benny. Her revelations appeared under the lurid headline 'I Was Benny's Love-

Slave', but even she insisted that their relationship stopped short of full sexual intercourse. It was not an affair in the accepted sense of the word.

Benny sometimes seemed to prefer to look but not touch. He loved going to girlie and strip shows and staring at the women on offer in the windows of Amsterdam and Hamburg. He knew the red-light districts intimately in every city he went to. Whenever he went to Australia, he stopped off for a few days in Bangkok, to take advantage of the city's notorious massage parlours and girlie bars. He made no secret of his predilection for massage parlours. He thought it was perfectly normal acceptable behaviour as long as you were a bachelor. If you were unmarried, it did not matter what you did because you were not betraying a partner.

If you were married, it was different. He was quite prudish about this. He once described a holiday he had spent in Hamburg with a pal. 'It really was fun,' he told me. 'We went running up and down the Reeperbahn like a couple of football hooligans. We went in all the beerhalls, we conducted the band, we went in the strip shows, I felt about seventeen and I think he felt about twelve.' Then he added sternly: 'You mustn't tell anyone about this, because he's a married man, you know.'

He loved Bangkok – until the eighties when he became too famous to be anonymous any more. 'The last time I was there,' he told me, 'I went to a disco. I had been into all sorts of other places, but I hadn't actually been into a disco. They are really just bars, full of these very small Thai ladies, all under five foot. I thought I'd better try so I went to the Grand Prix, which I was told was supposed to be the best. It was ninety degrees outside, but when you went in the perspiration froze on your face because the air-conditioning was so cold. The music was going thud, thud, thud, girls were either in little evening dresses or bikinis. I went in and this little lady says, "Oh come here." So I bought her a drink. The music's going, people were gyrating, and I was just getting used to the light. I sat down. The place was choc-a-bloc with girls, not many customers, and she suddenly said, "You the so. You may sew." '

It took Benny a while to realize that she was saying: 'You make show,' on TV. In fact, the penny only dropped when she raised her little hand in a Fred Scuttle salute. 'So of course all the girls had to come over, and there were about twenty of them, all getting excited because there was someone they'd actually seen on TV in their bar,' he said. 'They couldn't believe it. I didn't stay too long. I thought, "I've got to get out of here, it's all a bit much." But they all kissed me goodbye, one after the other all over the face, and I got outside, and I'd got to get back to the Oriental Hotel. So I wiped my face a bit with my handkerchief and it was solid with lipstick, every colour under the sun.' He beamed at the memory.

During that trip he was asked to do some interviews in Bangkok, one with an English-speaking woman of feminist views. 'She was giving me a hard time,' he said. 'I asked her if she thought my shows were anti-women, and she had to admit she had never seen one. She kept on saying, "Why you come to Bangkok?" I said it's a beautiful city, and I haven't been here for nearly twenty years. She asked me again, "Why you come, why you come?" Of course, she wanted me to say for the women, but I wasn't going to say that.'

He suddenly added: 'What is the answer to places like Bangkok? It's very sad the way a country like Thailand is run. A girl has a choice between being a prostitute, or almost starving to death. It's really very sad.' It was about the most thoughtful thing I ever heard him say about women.

The rest of the time he talked publicly about the opposite sex as if they were playthings. I once observed him as he watched a girl dancing, and his tongue hung down to his chin much as it did when he contemplated a cream cake. His idea of bliss was to be the one man wallowing in a positive sea of female flesh. He told me about an incident when he was in Australia.

'A girl who worked on the hotel switchboard phoned up and said, "Would you like to come to a party? My brother is dying to meet you." I said, "Look, I'm tired of meeting men, how about a party to meet some girls?" She said "Right!" And she produced them. There were no other men at the party, just me and seventeen girls.' This was his ideal. Especially if people knew about it. He did not party in stealth.

Because he remained so resolutely unmarried and had no regular girlfriend, the rumours that he was gay continued for years. This made it even more important to him that his public really believed that he was constantly surrounded by the most beautiful girls in his private life, just as he was in his shows. Often, of course, he was. But usually he had just invited them to tea to talk about their careers. He would get them to walk outside on the balcony of the Queensgate flat so that the world would know that they were there.

'I sometimes think the people across the road mustn't know what to make of me, all alone here,' he said, 'so when I have a girl for dinner or when some of the girls from the show call round, I joke, "You must go outside and walk up and down a bit on the balcony." I'm afraid the people over there will think I'm strange if I don't walk out with a woman from time to time.' On that occasion, he even got me to stroll outside with him for a few minutes.

Then it would be back to the jokes again. 'To tell the truth, there were some girls staying across the road there one time and they sent a note across saying, "Can we come over?" I note it's always we and not I, but I'm not complaining because if I fall asleep they can always talk to each other! I imagine people also think that I'm having it off with the girls in my show. Well I haven't had it off with them since ... what time is it now?' Then he would look pointedly at his watch.

Sometimes the joke would be at his own expense. He'd leap up, seize an address book and announce: 'This is the book where I keep the names of all the girls I've been to bed with. They're in alphabetical order. Starting with Zelda ...'

His relationship with the girls he worked with was genuinely more professional than anything else. One Hill's Angel did tell a newspaper that he had touched and groped her, but everyone on the show agreed it was a lie. 'There simply wasn't a word of truth in it,' said Bob Todd. Benny treated them all with the utmost circumspection. 'I suppose it's like a fatherly interest I have in them,' he told me. 'I give them advice about their careers, but they never take it. They prefer to listen to their boyfriends who always seem to be used-car salesmen, or plumbers. I despair sometimes because there's some real talent there and they won't listen.'

At rehearsals he would tell them: 'Don't read a book, don't do your knitting, watch Henry, watch Toddy. You can learn something. I'm totally wrapped up in work, you see.' He'd gesture arund him and add: 'Of all the books in this flat, there isn't one that isn't about show-business. Everything you see lying around, every photo, every bit of paper, is to do with work.' And that was about as close to the truth as he ever got.

He was totally obsessed with work, to the point where it is impossible to imagine any woman being happily married to him. She would have had to be a saint and a psychiatrist. He had no capacity for deep and meaningful relationships, or for the occasional tedium of marriage. Life to him was always like a first date. And probably because he'd had no success in persuading anyone to marry him, he pretended to be very disillusioned about marriage in general. 'In my case, I just don't think marriage is a good idea,' he would say. 'A third of all marriages end in divorce, and a third stay together because of the children, so only a third work.'

Another of his favourite lines was that he had the mentality of a seventeen-year-old and seventeen was far too young to get married. Perhaps he was nearer to the truth than he intended. His attitude to sex, all enthusiasm, cheerful boasting and outward show, was very much that of a teenager. To the end of his life, he referred to himself as a boy and all women as girls or young ladies.

From the mid-sixties, probably dating from his rejected proposal to Annette André, Benny never admitted to falling in love again. Instead he started creating an image for himself as the man always surrounded by girls – one girl was never enough – which continued right up to his death. Sometimes he used the girls from the show as cover for the fact that he didn't actually have a real girlfriend. He won many awards, and sometimes could be persuaded to go to the ceremony to collect them. He once asked Jenny Lee-Wright to be his escort to one grand awards dinner at the Café Royal.

'My boyfriend at the time was furious I'd accepted, because we were supposed to be at some party in Oxford.

I told him it would not be good to say no, so we arranged that I would leave at midnight and get to Oxford to join him. I had to tell Benny I was going to do a Cinderella on him. He was terribly nervous about having to say a few words of acceptance, he'd got it all mapped out and kept going over and over it. Just when he got to the important bit of the evening, I upped and left him on his own. He never invited me to anything like that again! But I think he was used to that sort of thing. All the girls on the show were in love with their boyfriends. He told me there'd been a couple of women he'd loved who'd turned him down, or left him, and I think he had made a decision to be on his own from then on. But I wouldn't have described him as lonely.'

On other social occasions, he liked to be accompanied by more than one of the girls from his show. Bob Todd recalls: 'If ever there was a party or a reception, he would sit in a corner with half a dozen of the Hill's Angels around him. He seemed to use them as a wall between himself and the rest of the world.' Having created the image as the man all other men envied, he believed in it so fervently that he hated to be photographed alone. Benny Hill must not be seen to be on his own, unless he was dressed as Fred Scuttle when it was OK. He had to have a girl in the picture. Preferably two. He saw himself as a Parisian boulevardier with a girl on either arm. So he started using any public occasion as a double opportunity.

It would be a photo-opportunity so he could get his picture into the papers with a couple of young lovelies in tow. But he could also use the chance to vet new girls who had applied to join the show or had been suggested by his choreographer. It was an unnofficial audition. Talking and listening to them throughout a meal would give him some idea of what they could do and how serious they were about their careers.

This happened when Thames held a lavish lunch at London's Savoy Hotel in January 1983 to celebrate getting their franchise renewed. A couple of hopefuls had been invited to sit with Benny so that he could chat to them about their qualifications and ambitions and see if he thought they might be good enough for the show. On the way in, he was photographed with one of them, who succeeded in giving reporters the impression that she was the new serious girlfriend in Benny's life.

Indeed she may have thought she was in with a chance when he clutched her hand throughout most of the lunch and leaned on her thigh occasionally. But from where I was sitting at the same table, it looked as though he was doing it to help keep himself upright. It was a long and fairly embarrassing occasion – someone got carried away and started heckling the speakers including Eric More-cambe – and the Savoy's finest wines were flowing. Benny was thoroughly drunk. At the end of the affair, he was helped into his car by Dennis Kirkland, who had to go home with him to make sure he got safely to bed. The girl went home alone.

The same thing happened at a couple of Thames' famous garden parties which they held at the end of each summer. All their artists would be invited, but Benny usually turned the invitations down. Then one year he said he would go provided a couple of girls were also invited for him to be photographed with, and audition at the same time.

At the 1986 party there was one poor girl who was desperate to get on TV. At the end of the afternoon, I heard her urging him: 'You will phone me, won't you? Please! I will hear from you? Promise?' She must have been all of eighteen. She may well have heard from Benny again, but she never got on to the show.

Towards the end of his life, he was less driven by sex, and replaced it with a genuine enjoyment of the company of pretty girls, the younger and more impressionable the better. But their company was literally all he wanted. He was re-creating once again that early image of the comic surrounded by girls, loved by all who looked at him.

8

Friendship

It was after one of his more painful rejections that Benny turned to two other women whose friendship was eventually to mean far more to him than ephemeral relationships with various glamorous girls. Bizarrely, for a man obsessed with physical beauty, they were women for whom glamour was an impossibility. Both were severely handicapped and confined to wheelchairs. Yet with them he forged two of the deepest relationships of his life. Perhaps at last he felt safe from being rejected.

Benny was meticulous about answering fan-mail. Even though he had no help except in the early days, and the backlog of letters which piled up usually looked far too daunting ever to be sorted out, they would all get an answer in the end. He cared passionately about his fans, and would answer everything by hand. Moreover he would remember the details of each letter. For some years he had been corresponding with several fans who had one thing in common. They all suffered from cerebral palsy. On and off, there were five of these women, though by the time he told me about them, three had died.

He kept these friendships very quiet. But every now and again, when they were in the middle of pre-production work on the next batch of shows, he would give Dennis Kirkland a phone number in Leicester and say: 'If you need me at all, I'll be at this number for the next few days.' On other occasions it would be a number in Felixstowe, Suffolk. It took a long time for even Kirkland to prise out of him where he was going – to visit the two women he referred to as 'the girls', Netta Warner and Phoebe King.

One day in 1983, he suddenly decided to tell me about his secret visits but he was petrified it would sound as if he was boasting about his good works. He kept saying: 'I hate that "Look at me, I'm dancing" attitude,' referring to people who deliberately draw attention to their good works. 'I do my fair share for charity, but I don't want an OBE or anything like that,' he went on. 'I'm quite happy sitting here quietly. Virtue is its own reward. Or so they tell me.'

He was quite adamant that he did not visit Netta and Phoebe just as a charitable act. He enjoyed the visits every bit as much as they did. He received from the pair a totally unconditional friendship and affection he apparently couldn't find anywhere else.

He had first met Phoebe King in 1952 when she was sixteen. Her grandparents brought her backstage at one of his Sunday night concerts in Felixstowe, Suffolk. They were waiting at the stagedoor when Benny came out, asked for his autograph and introduced him to the young girl in the wheelchair. Her mother had been killed in the Blitz, and she was then cared for by her grandparents. When they died, she moved into the sheltered accommodation in Walton, Felixstowe in which she still lives. After that first meeting, Benny never forgot her. He started writing to her and whenever he was on his travels, would send her postcards from all over the world. They were invariably addressed to 'Kitten' and signed 'Love, Teddy'.

Netta Warner lived in Wigston, Leicester with her parents. She died only a few weeks before Benny, still cared for at home by her eighty-year-old mother Nell. A few years younger than Phoebe, Netta started writing to Benny in 1957, sending him a card for his thirty-third birthday. He wrote back to her just as he would to any fan, without knowing that she was handicapped.

One day he noticed her phone number on the top of another letter and decided to surprise her with a call. After that they spoke on the phone several times, but she did not mention her disability. 'I talked to her quite a few times without knowing she was spastic,' he told me. 'She just didn't mention it. It really impressed me.' He only found out later that she spent all her waking hours in a wheelchair.

Her real name was Jeanette. 'But chosen ones are allowed to call her Netta,' Benny said fondly.

On one particular day in the late sixties, Benny had been feeling extremely low and depressed, he said. 'I was going through a really rotten patch and feeling very sorry for myself,' he told me. Then he pulled himself together. After all, he was rich, famous and healthy. He had so much going for him. 'I thought this is really silly. There are a lot of people worse off than you,' he said. 'So I found Phoebe's number at her grandparents', phoned up and said, "How would you like me to come up and see you?"' Naturally she said yes, and Benny set off on the first of his many expeditions to Felixstowe which were to go on for over twenty years.

'I first went up there for the day,' he said, 'and didn't even think of staying overnight. But the grandparents said, "Next time you come, you must stay." So I did. They all lived in quite a nice house then, and I would stay with them. I have been going up to see her every year since then.'

Soon afterwards he made the same offer of a visit to Netta, and was equally welcome. Netta lived with her parents in a much smaller house, so Benny would stay in a motel about two miles away.

'Netta's condition is that much worse than Phoebe's,' he said, 'so she is stuck with four walls all day. She can't get about as much as Phoebe.' Neither of them got out very much, in fact, because the wheelchairs were so heavy to manoeuvre. Not everyone could manage them. Even Benny, tall and strong, claimed he had to get into training before each visit.

Then he decided to invite the girls to London. To make things as easy as possible, he did a recce beforehand to find out which theatres and which hotels had either ramps or lifts which would accommodate wheelchairs. He could easily have asked someone else to get this information for him, but he seemed to get a special pleasure out of doing it himself.

Netta's first outing to London was to see *My Fair Lady*. 'I don't think she had ever been outside Leicester before, never mind to London. I thought it all might be a bit too much for her, but somehow we managed it. I took her to the Savoy for lunch before the show and it was a great success,' he said. Then Phoebe came to London and was pushed around the Serpentine, and treated to a similar slap-up lunch.

He continued bringing the pair to London occasionally until they both became too infirm to make the journey. And he went to visit each of them at their homes regularly every year. In the eighties, it became like a Grand Tour for him each summer: a week with Netta, a week with Phoebe, followed by several days with his favourite Hill's

Angela, Sue Upton, and her family. Then, finally, a visit to his beloved Aunt Louie at Bexleyheath.

Benny admitted that the whole thing with Phoebe and Netta had begun as an act of charity on his part, but developed into something far more valuable. 'It started off as a sense of duty,' he said. 'You've got to give back a little in this world. You can't just take all the time, and I have so much.' But then he found he enjoyed it every bit as much as they did. 'It wasn't just doing good works. It's no longer a thing I do because it's good for my soul. I do it because I enjoy their company. I mean, they are really nice to talk to, they are both very sensible and wise.'

There could be no question of a romance or physical relationship with them because of their handicaps. The friendships were always just friendships. Mrs Brenda Garrison, warden of the sheltered housing where Phoebe now lives, describes the relationship between Benny and Phoebe as being more like brother and sister than any-thing else. And perhaps because there was no question of romance, the absence of sexual tension allowed Benny to relax with 'the girls' more than he could with anyone else. They were, by force of circumstances, a very unworldly pair, and provided a sort of refuge for him, totally removed from the showbusiness world. He told me that he seriously thought he was closer to the two of them than to anyone else in the world. 'Very, very close,' he said.

Much of his initial feeling for them sprang from his admiration for their courage and optimism. He knew he could never have the same sort of courage himself. After his first heart attack in February 1992, his greatest fear was that he would be incapacitated and have to rely totally on other people. But Netta's and Phoebe's attitude also provided a dramatic contrast to the sort of girls he had been going out with, actresses and dancers whose careers depended so much on the way they looked.

'The odd thing is,' he mused, 'that it's the pretty girls who are going to be the suicides, when they lose their prettiness. It is not the blind person or the handicapped person, they have no self-pity. Netta is amazing, how high her spirits are under the circumstances. They are both very brave and wonderful women, I admire them tremendously. They have this terrible handicap. I have got to cope with it for five days or so when I go to see them, they have got it for ever.'

He lavished gifts and flowers on both women. Netta's mother, Mrs Nell Warner, described how Benny would tell her to get anything that Netta needed to make her life a little more pleasant, and he would pay for it. 'He'd say, "It doesn't matter what it costs, just get it." He was very good to us,' she said. 'He did his best to make us comfortable.'

Benny was also interested in trying to make Netta do something for herself. He saw how she made tablecloths and bedspreads, but he also believed that she had the talent to make it in his own field, as a comedy writer. 'I've tried like mad to get Netta interested in writing,' he told me, 'because she really is very bright. She has a great sense of humour, a real sense of comedy. Sometimes she'll come out with some very funny put-downs. She'll make a funny remark and get a bigger laugh than I get! Sometimes I tease her and say, "But I get paid for it, you don't. So I'm trying to get her interested in writing instead of just sitting in her room doing nothing. I tell her, it is just possible that in three or four years' time, Morecambe and Wise could be writing to you, asking "Where is the new material? We need more material."' Benny was quite serious about trying to teach her to write sketches. He said: 'She knows all the jokes. I feel like putting a stick of dynamite behind her to make her write something down and actually do something with her humour.'

He also took her horse-racing. At the time of her death, he'd been trying to plan a surprise outing to the races for her, arranging for a driver to go all the way to Leicester to fetch her and take her home.

Phoebe was financially more comfortable than Netta. When her grandparents died, she was left alone in the world, but somehow her personality blossomed, he said. In 1972, she moved into Conford House, Walton, where she has a bedsitter with its own kitchen and bathroom.

Benny did not pay for her upkeep. 'I don't care for her in the financial sense, she is not broke,' he said. 'She lives in this very nice complex, very nice indeed, warm and comfortable. She is very lucky in many ways compared to some people with the same handicap.' But Mrs Garrison says that Benny was generous instead with his time and thoughtfulness. The postcards would pour in. Beautiful bouquets would arrive with a message saying, 'In case you need cheering up', or 'Just something to brighten your day'.

For all the comfort of Conford House, Phoebe does not have much of a life. She goes out rarely. Her wheelchair is too much for many people to push, since cerebral palsy victims tend to grow heavy through lack of exercise. She has someone who comes in to clean and wash for her, and another who comes in to help bath her and the other twenty-odd residents, both part of the community nursing service. Sometimes she will ask the cleaner or the bath lady to go out to lunch with her. She'll say: 'I'll pay for a taxi if you come with me.'

Occasionally, if a bus is available which can accommodate wheelchairs, the residents are taken on an outing.

Phoebe has also been taken to visit a cousin in Bournemouth. But apart from that, life in Conford House differs
very little from one day to the next. So Benny's visits
naturally became very important indeed to Phoebe, literally the highspot of her year. She used to fantasize that
she was a princess, and for one week each year, she really
felt like one.

He would usually arrive by taxi, with his things in his
customary assortment of carrier bags, and stay in
the Conford House guest room. He used some of his
time there to write for the show. The rest he devoted
entirely to Phoebe. He pushed her along the front in
her wheelchair. He took her to a restaurant for lunch
or dinner every day. For the meals when they didn't go
out, the pair of them cooked something in Phoebe's little
kitchen.

'She does an awful lot for herself,' he told me, 'and I
let her do it because that's what she wants. I could do all
the washing up while I'm there for instance, or get all the
meals, but she doesn't want that. She wants to cook for
me. Some of the other ladies there offer to do things for
me, too, my washing or my ironing. I get very spoiled
there.'

During his week-long visit, he would always make a
point of taking the cleaner and the bath lady out to lunch
as well, as a thank you for helping take care of Phoebe.
And when he left he would present Phoebe with a bottle
of champagne. Each year, she kept it until New Year's
Eve, then shared it with the other residents. 'We'd all toast
him and say, "Happy New Year, Benny",' said Brenda
Garrison. 'Phoebe liked to remember him that way, and
she also got pleasure out of contributing the champagne
to the party.'

Phoebe would send Benny a bowl of plants for Valentine's Day. Among the gifts he bought her was a small dress ring. But the friendship remained platonic.

He could not explain exactly why the friendships meant so much to him, or why he felt able to talk so freely to the two invalids. 'I tell them my troubles to a certain extent,' he said, 'but I only tell them things I think they should know, not the troubles I don't think they should be worried with.'

Brenda Garrison thinks that it was just that he was able to relax in their company: 'They weren't treating him as if he was a star, they treated him as a person. They were able to relate to him in a perfectly normal way, out of the sort of limelight he was used to. Nothing that he ever said to them would ever go beyond the four walls. He trusted them.'

9

The Top of the Tree

In 1968 Benny had been lured from the BBC over to ATV by Lew Grade to make a series at ATV's Elstree studios. In those days, the company specialized in a sort of mid-Atlantic entertainment which was supposed to appeal to audiences in both Britain and the States, but which often fell somewhere in the middle wilderness.

Benny agreed because there was the possibility that he could break into the American market via this route. ATV were also offering more money. But he had little control over the content of the show, which he hated. He had to do sketches with American artists who were sometimes big stars, so Benny's wishes were not paramount. 'Frankly, the shows were dreadful,' said Richard Stone. 'Benny was terribly unhappy.' As Richard drove him back down the A1 into London after the final show, Benny said: 'That's it. I'm never going back to Elstree again.'

But where to go next? Back to the BBC? Or pastures new? Stone thought of the newly-created Thames Television, which had the London weekday franchise. A hybrid of the old ABC and Rediffusion outfits, merged into one by the Independent Television Authority, it began life with only a handful of programmes carried on from the two former companies. The head of its Light Entertainment department was Philip Jones, whose only previous contact with Benny had been as producer of the famous sixties' pop programme 'Thank Your Lucky Stars', where artists mimed to their latest releases. Benny had one of his unlikely record hits with a recitation called *Pepys' Diary*, and duly mimed it for Philip.

Now Jones was looking for talent. Thames were required to produce over one hundred hours a year of light entertainment for the whole ITV network. Philip began a tradition of Thames situation comedies which would eventually include hits like 'Father Dear Father', 'Bless This House', 'Man About the House', 'Love Thy Neighbour', 'Robin's Nest', 'George and Mildred', and many more. But he also needed a second strand of variety shows. One of the most popular men in British television, he succeeded beyond his wildest dreams. A few years later, you could walk through the restaurant block on any day and see Eric Morecambe and Ernie Wise, Benny Hill, Eamonn Andrews, Des O'Connor, Mike Yarwood, Tommy Cooper, Eric Sykes, Jim Davidson and other top artists all working for Thames. But in 1968 he was starting almost from scratch. 'So when the Benny Hill offer came along from Richard, it was grabbed with all hands,' he said. 'Little did we know it at the time, but it spearheaded everything else we did in variety.'

Benny never signed one of the long-term contracts many artists are bound by. Each year, he and Philip would discuss how many shows he wanted to do. The most ever was five; sometimes only three. It depended on how much material Benny felt he had, and on studio availability. Thames used to have what they called 'blackboard meetings' every quarter, where the facilities department would mark up on the blackboard what studios and what film crews were available. Drama and Light Entertainment wrangled amiably over Studio One, Thames' largest. Philip would put his name down for it, with his fingers crossed that Benny would have the material to justify the booking.

But Benny could not be forced to write or brought to the brink by any outside influences. Ultimately it was always down to him, and the company happily went along with whatever he felt he had to offer. Philip just had to second-guess him each time. 'He would ring up and say, "Well, there's definitely three but can you bear with me, because there might be four," so it was a bit of a balancing act.'

The early shows were more like old-fashioned variety with musical numbers by guest artists interspersed with the sketches, but Benny gradually phased them out. Philip would have preferred him to lean a little more on guests in order to preserve the most valuable commodity, his own comedy material, but Benny managed to cope with the pressure of providing more and more for each show. The cleverness of some of his ideas was later over-shadowed by the sexy image of his shows, which was a shame. It was not all sauce.

Benny had a solid grounding in slapstick and seaside postcard humour, and he was one of the first comics to get material out of the fallacies of the film and television industry. His bespectacled idiot, Fred Scuttle, appeared in the guise of film producer, director, TV star and TV director. The characterization was sharp enough to make people in the industry roar with recognition, and broad enough to make the audience at home laugh too.

Inept continuity, such as someone having a tie on one second and being tie-less the next, was a favourite target, as was bad direction, with the camera cutting too soon to things it shouldn't have seen. There was a famous sketch where he played a *grande dame* being interviewed for a

Playing one of his many female characters with Jon Jon Keefe in 1975 (*Jon Jon Keefe*).

A rare outing to pick up a Variety Club award as ITV Personality of 1979, with Penelope Keith, BBC Personality and Tommy Steele, Showbusiness Personality (*Press Association*).

The many faces of Benny Hill (*Scope Features*).

Eurovision link-up. There was a sound delay on the line, so that she kept answering the question before last. This idea has been extended and elaborated by many other comedy writers, but Benny was surely the first to use it.

Benny was mocked in later years for the amount of time he spent watching TV, including the whole of Christmas, but it certainly paid off. 'Watching television and films was his life,' said Philip, 'and the parodies which he produced as a result were always greatly underrated. The people who slagged him off in the latter years were terribly unfair to the quality of his material.' In fact, one of the comics who was most critical of Benny regularly used in his own BBC series a device where the camera was turned upside down for close-ups, so that people's chins became their foreheads, and vice versa. Benny had done the same trick years earlier.

His Thames shows were instantly successful. Because they were shown spasmodically rather than as a consecutive weekly series, they became a television event, and frequently hit the No. 1 spot in the TV ratings, with audiences sometimes exceeding twenty million. By now this was the only work he did. He concentrated his whole being on the shows. He became a pure television animal and an absolute master of his craft.

Where some comedians are content just to turn up and do the material they are given, Benny wanted total control. He had come to Thames with the idea that he might even be allowed to direct his own shows, but union rules put paid to that. Instead he kept a beady eye on the directors and producers he was given. He liked to be included in the editing and dubbing of the shows, arriving in the editing suite with a couple of bottles of red wine and a pile of Mars Bars for a day's hard work. It took more than tact to overrule his suggestions. It took professional diplomacy. He was no pussycat to work with. 'He was pernickety but not difficult,' said Philip. 'There was no real abrasion while he was working, but he would moan afterwards that they hadn't read the script properly. He'd say, "I wanted six-inch treads on the stairs for this gag and they gave me eight inches. It was right there in the script. And I said I wanted this costume cut away just so, and I wanted Velcro down the back of that one, and they didn't give it to me. Why don't they just read what I've put in the script?" He wouldn't make an unpleasant thing of it, but it would certainly be something he'd want to discuss with me the next time we met.'

Benny would phone to make a date to come in to see Philip, and ask for assurances that these little mistakes wouldn't happen again. But he would never hold up the production because of them. So sometimes the back-up team would produce four or five wigs, and five different hats, rather than be caught out with something that Benny did not like, all of which ultimately had an effect on the cost of the show.

In the early days, Benny and his 'boss' went out for regular meals together. But although they were such good friends and colleagues for twenty years, Philip never felt that he really got to know Benny. 'We would discuss what we'd seen on TV or in shows, or were about to see, and what we'd both liked or disliked. But he wasn't easy to talk to. I had no insights into his private life whatever.'

Like Richard and Sara Stone, Philip and his wife Florence worried about Benny being alone at Christmas. 'We invited him a couple of times. I said, "Do feel free to come round, just come when you want to, go to sleep when you want to, disappear whenever you want to." But the invitations were politely declined. He just preferred to be on his own.' Eventually, even the restaurant trips stopped.

'He was totally accessible if I wanted to talk to him but we didn't have many things to talk about. That's not to say I didn't like and admire him enormously. I did. But I didn't have an easy social relationship with him. I think the only person Benny was socially at ease with was Dennis Kirkland.'

Benny had several different producers and directors over the years. He won a prestigious BAFTA award for Best Light Entertainment in 1971, for a show produced and directed by John Robbins and David Bell. It was the first of eleven major awards he would harvest while with Thames. But despite the success of the end product, Benny's dealings with his different mentors were not always easy.

Jon Jon Keefe, who was in the shows from 1973, remembers quite a few 'fights'. Not that Benny ever lost his temper and shouted. Everyone just knew the star was unhappy when he started picking at his nails and fingertips, and whistling to himself. 'That was the sign to head for cover,' said Jon Jon. Sometimes when Benny got very cross, his fingertips would be picked till they bled, and he would come in at the end of the week with every finger covered with sticking plaster.

At one point, he was given a gay director, one of the most talented men in the light entertainment field. At an early stage during rehearsals, Benny suddenly excused himself to go to the Gents, and gestured to Dennis Kirkland, then working as floor manager, to join him there.

'Is he what I think he is?' he demanded. 'Yes,' said Kirkland, 'why?' 'I can't work with him,' protested Benny. It wasn't that he had any objection to gays. He just thought the man would be incapable of understanding the whole ethos of the show, the saucy sexual innuendo, the boy-chases-girl element, what made a girl look tantalizing and what didn't. But they went on to make two shows together and they were just as successful as the rest.

Benny's problems were alleviated when Dennis Kirkland was promoted from floor manager to producer/director status and began to make series with top comics like Ken Dodd and Tommy Cooper.

Benny and Kirkland had long been friends. Dennis was one of the most easygoing men imaginable. He never stopped laughing and had a good understanding of comedy. He had once been a warm-up comic in his spare time, and some people had tried to persuade him to take it up professionally. Now Benny wanted him to take over his show. 'Dennis was a great support for comics, he genuinely liked their jokes and had a great ability to show it,' said Philip Jones. It was a mutual decision between Philip and Benny when Kirkland was at last given responsibility for the show. 'There were hesitations in both our minds at first, and then the time came when we both thought Den was ready for it,' said Philip. Benny never looked back.

Kirkland was on his wavelength to such an extent that all the old troubles about ideas being wrongly executed melted away. Communication between them was almost telepathic. 'Dennis could interpret Benny's shorthand both on the page and in his mind,' said Philip. 'It worked very, very well.'

Jon Jon Keefe said: 'Kirkland was invaluable to him because they were so tuned in, they didn't fight. He knew how to motivate Benny and how to persuade him and also when to shut up and accept what Benny said. With some of the others, you could see the tension in Benny. But he and Dennis never lost their rags. Kirkland may have ultimately made the show more expensive, but that was because he concentrated totally on the person who was saying what he wanted. I think he got to the end result more easily in many ways than some of the others. The overheads kept going up but Den always came through with the goods.'

Benny's Thames shows were sold to most countries in Europe and many other parts of the world. By the time he left the company, the total had reached eighty-four. Benny was half pleased, half regretful because it curtailed the free and easy anonymous travel he loved. 'Travelling all over the world like I do has been a little more difficult since the show has been sold to so many countries,' he complained. 'There's a problem with people inviting me to things all the time, not because they think you will enjoy yourself but because they think you will provide the entertainment. They look upon you as a free cabaret and I get a bit fed up.' He claimed that at one meal there was a revolting small boy who tape-recorded every sound emanating from Benny, including the sound of him crunching his celery and radishes.

He could no longer move so easily in his beloved France and Spain. 'I was in Paris for a boxing match,' he told me, 'and in the middle of the fight I got swamped by people and knocked to the ground. They were jumping in my lap trying to take photos of me in the middle of the match!'

The next night he had gone to see the legendary existentialist singer, Juliette Greco, and this time he wanted to be spotted. He was longing to meet her. He hoped she'd see him and ask him round for a drink. 'But when you want to be recognized, you just never are. Just my luck.'

Even Madrid was getting a bit hairy for him, he said. It was now difficult for him to visit all the little theatres and circuses he loved without detracting attention from the performers. 'Every theatre I went in last time I was there, I was announced from the stage within five minutes. When there was a singer on, the kids all came running to get my autograph which wasn't very nice for the person trying to do the singing. But if you don't do it, the kids' feelings are hurt, so life gets very difficult.'

One market, however, eluded Thames until the mid-seventies. Try as they might they could not get American TV to buy the show. British comedians had traditionally failed in America, and it looked as if Benny was going to follow suit.

Then a super-successful American businessman called Don Taffner stepped into the frame. Don was the middle-man who had sold many of Thames sit-coms to the States, and had made the company a fortune by selling the format rights to shows like 'Man About the House'. The Americans then made their own version with their own stars. Now he asked Philip Jones whether there was any other product he might be able to sell and Philip told him about Benny. After looking at the shows, Don decided they would be much more viable for the US market if they were in half-hour form. Richard Stone suggested the name of John Street, who had been one of Benny's favourite producers at the BBC but was now retired. John was not only a famously skilled editor, but very familiar with Benny's work. So John was hired to distil and edit some half-hours from all the material so far available. His first half-hour was transferred from the British 625-line system to the American 525, and shown by Don Taffner at a major trade fair held by the National Association of Television Programme Executives in Los Angeles. Don had one definite commitment from a station in Phila-delphia, but needed more to make the edits financially viable. An executive at the Philadelphia station made a brave decision to 'strip' the shows, showing them on five consecutive nights. This would use up an awful lot of material very fast. In fact, they weren't arriving from London fast enough, and the station initially showed the same few over and over again. But the ploy worked. Other stations swiftly bought the show, with a New York channel at one point screening it twice nightly. Soon the whole of America was talking about Benny Hill. If you were a British visitor in the States there was only one thing people wanted to know: 'You're English? Say, do you know Benny Hill?'

The shows were eventually sold to a hundred different stations, and are still being bought by seventy-five today.

Possibly the most remarkable thing about all this was the deal Richard Stone had negotiated for Benny regarding sales to America. He got fifty per cent of everything Thames received, a contract probably unique in British television. Now the money poured in faster than ever, and Benny's millions began to accumulate. 'He didn't make all that much before the American deal, because he did no live work for so long,' said Richard Stone. His fee for each show was not particularly high and just doing three or four shows a year wasn't going to make him mega-rich. For that he'd have needed to do summer seasons, cabaret, films and all the rest. 'He was probably on about £100,000 a year,' said Richard. 'But the American deal changed all that for ever.' Without lifting a finger, except to advise on editing the shows for America, Benny made millions.

The man who had made all this possible, and was also becoming rather rich as a result, naturally wanted to meet the golden goose. 'But throughout the early years, I never did get to meet Benny,' Don Taffner remembered. 'I'm not saying this harshly, but it was almost as if Thames didn't want us to meet each other. Every time I was in London, there were always reasons why it didn't happen. They would say he was out of town or something, and it all became kind of embarrassing. I think Philip was as embarrassed as I was.'

In fact, Philip Jones was making strenuous efforts to bring the pair together. He'd invite Benny to go out to dinner with the Taffners, and Benny would ask how many people would be there. Only five or six, Philip would assure him. But Benny would still prevaricate. 'Do I have to?' he'd whine, like a child told to come in and meet his parents' guests.

In the end they did meet and became friends. Don had a background in vaudeville which fascinated Benny. He also became very close to Don's wife Eleanor. 'They bumped into one another one day in Marks and Spencer's in Oxford Street,' Don recalled. 'She was buying under-pants for me and Benny was buying them for himself, and from that moment they were pals. He used to talk to her a lot and tell her about his mother and his childhood. We never found Benny difficult to talk to, though strangely enough it was easier if Dennis wasn't there. When Dennis was around, it was jokes all the way. Their patter was halfway between scripted and natural, almost as if they had rehearsed it. When Benny was on his own you could talk to him about ordinary things, and I found him terrific and fascinating.' And, as Don points out, the friendship was founded on a big financial success. 'And that's a strong foundation.'

It was, indeed, a very strong foundation. Thanks to sales of 'The Benny Hill Show' and other Thames pro-grammes including the documentary series 'The World at War', Thames won the Queen's Award for Export Achievement in 1984, the first broadcaster to be so honoured. There was one financial year when foreign sales of 'The Benny Hill Show' were said to be the only reason the parent company actually ended up making a profit.

The shows cost far more than normal light entertainment programmes. By the late eighties, the budget had reached over £500,000 for each hour-long programme, compared to an average cost in 1989 for light entertainment of less than £200,000 per hour. It was largely due to Benny's increasing the scope of the sketches in his writing, requiring more and more time for outside filming. The cost of scenery, props and special effects was also going up. Because Benny played so many characters, the whole studio would often be kept waiting while he was in make-up being turned into Liz Taylor or whoever for the next bit of the sketch. There was very little they could do without him because he dominated the action.

Benny's insistence on having everyone in the cast on hand for the whole two or three weeks of location filming was also very expensive. Sometimes people would sit around for days with little to do, but Benny wanted them all there just in case. 'If Thames had been unhappy about the cost,' said agent Richard Stone, 'I would have expected them to sit down and talk about it and suggest perhaps that he didn't need to have all the girls there every single day.' But no one ever did.

The expense could not officially be discounted against overseas sales. Those belonged to a sister company, Thames Television International, with a separate balance sheet. 'You could never use overseas revenue as an argument within the department if anyone moaned about the budget,' said Philip Jones. 'But I'm quite certain that at boardroom level, if someone said, "I see costs of 'The Benny Hill Show' are fifteen per cent up," someone else would point out that they were getting the money back, and much more, from overseas. We did everything we could to keep down the costs, and I'm sure behind closed doors, the budget was happily accepted.' Philip felt that the unique quality of the end product justified the price. After all, it was Thames' most successful show. The irrepressible Kirkland was fond of swaggering round the studios joking to colleagues: 'Who pays your salaries round here? I do.'

10

The TV 'Family'

Benny liked to keep a tight grip on every aspect of the show, including the casting. Producers might tactfully suggest artists to him, but it was up to Benny in the end whether they stayed, or disappeared after one booking. It was important to him to have people he really got on with, and who got on with each other. The tight core of performers he kept around him for several years all loved and served him devotedly and referred to themselves as 'the family'.

Benny chose his cast for their ability to interpret his humour, and often for their extraordinary faces. He only had to look at Bob Todd to start laughing. Bob, known to everyone as Toddy, was a former RAF pilot with an impressive war record. He had turned gentleman farmer after the war, but yearned to be in showbusiness. At the age of forty-two, he decided it was now or never, and started hanging round the studios where the Tony Hancock shows were recorded, getting to know Hancock's writers and producer and passing himself off as an experienced actor. Nerve paid off, and though he never actually appeared in any edition of 'Hancock's Half Hour', he did get booked for a subsequent series starring Sid James.

He later appeared with many other comics, but set

himself the goal of working with the man he now considered to be the Number One TV comedian, Benny. 'I tried everything, I wrote letters, I turned up at the studios,' he said. 'I couldn't get near him. I dropped everything to try to get on "The Benny Hill Show". My optimism vanished and I was ready to give up the business. My family were really struggling.' But he got booked in the end. And the show wouldn't have been the same from that point on without Toddy's lugubrious face and even more lugubrious voice.

Nicholas Parsons was a 'straight' man with whom Benny could not keep a straight face, either. 'Benny found Nicholas hilarious,' said Bob. 'He would say if you want to see how to stretch out a bit part, watch Nicholas. There was a sketch where Benny and Jenny Lee-Wright were leaning on a ship's rail, and Nicholas just had to walk past and say: "Ah, I see we're slumming tonight, Jenny." And walk off. Benny was going, "Toddy, watch this, watch this." Nicholas came on, drew up beside them, paused; said, "Ah, Jenny." Paused, moved to the other side. "I see we are, er, ha-ha-ha," – another pause – "I see we are, er, slumming tonight. Ha-ha-ha!" And then slowly walked off. Benny was absolutely on his knees laughing, going, "Oh God, just look at him." We had such fun.'

There was another early sketch where Bob played a Pakistani ordering a meal in Benny's Chinese restaurant. Nicholas Parsons had to come on at the end as another customer. His only role in the sketch was to get a whole plate of chop suey over his head. 'When Nicholas came on he had his very own best suit on, his real "I am the master of ceremonies suit",' recalled Bob. 'Benny, the bugger, spotted it. He didn't do the chop suey on the head, he did it all over the precious suit, then nearly cried with laughter at Nick's face.'

Jackie Wright was the little bald Irishman whose head Benny used to pat like someone rapidly bouncing a ball. Jackie eventually became so popular that he had a fan club in the United States, and American TV offered him his own show. It is probably just as well he did not accept since it is doubtful if they would ever have understood a word he said, so broad was his Ulster accent.

Born in 1905, Jackie was one of twelve children and like his father and four of his brothers, had started his career as a body-builder in the car trade. He worked briefly for Cadillac in America at one point. Later he drifted into showbusiness, first as a trombonist, then as a film and TV extra.

He never married. For six months of the year he lived in a bedsitter in London. The other six he spent taking care of his invalid sister in Belfast. He once told me: 'I used to do quite well with the girls because I could tell a good tale, and had plenty of cheek. But now I've reached the age where I've no incentive to tell a tale at all.' He was about seventy-seven at the time.

Benny first met him when Jackie was hired as a non-speaking extra for one of his last BBC shows. He and Jackie hit it off straight away. Jackie couldn't act to save his life, but Benny recognized that his small stature, his sour, wrinkled face and his bald pate somehow added up to a very funny image. From that moment on, Benny never did a show without him.

At seventy-three, Jackie had tried to retire but was so bored after a few months, he wrote to Benny asking if he could come back. He was more than welcome. In his eighties Jackie became too ill to work and returned to Belfast, but even then Benny would insist on some left-over bit of footage of Jackie being included in as many shows as possible so that the little fellow would still get some money from the programme. He eventually died in 1989 and Benny mourned him deeply.

Henry McGee comes from a distinguished theatrical family going back to the eighteenth century. One of his ancestors, the actress Kitty Clive, had been a principal comedy player in David Garrick's company. Henry himself began his career as a spear carrier with the Comédie Française, but always claimed he wanted to play tragedy. In the end he bowed to the inevitable.

His elegant voice, suave manner and deadpan expression, even in the face of extreme provocation, made him an ideal straight man and he had become famous playing opposite Charlie Drake in a series called 'The Worker'. Shortly afterwards, Benny snapped him up and kept him for ever more. He thought Henry was the most versatile straight man he had ever had.

In 1973, Jon Jon Keefe was a good-looking East Ender with a fast line in chat and an accomplished showbusiness 'all-rounder'. He was working all round the West End, playing four clubs a night as singer, dancer, comic and compère. He used to start off at the Talk of the Town at 9.30 p.m., then off to L'Hirondelle at 10.30, then to a clip joint in Windmill Street for midnight, then back to L'Hirondelle in Swallow Street at 1.30 a.m.

One night at the Talk of the Town, he was told Benny Hill was in the audience with two girls. Afterwards, Benny sent a note round to Jon Jon, written on one of his usual bits of cheap lined paper, saying: 'Would you like to come on the show? Your enthusiasm and your joy in performing is something I think I could use in my next production.' Jon Jon said: 'Really I was just providing music to eat your soup by. I didn't expect to be noticed. There were terrible rumours at the time about Benny being gay, or AC/DC, so for several weeks I just ignored the note.'

When Jon Jon did pluck up courage to phone, Benny said he wanted him to sing a musical number with a girl and suggested he bring someone from the Talk of the Town. In those days, Benny's show still had several musical interludes between the comedy sketches. Jon Jon debated between taking a very beautiful girl who was musically a bit unsound, and one who was 'less of a looker' but sang very well. He took the one who could really sing. 'The irony was that the girl immediately appeared in several of Benny's shows, and I didn't get booked at first. I couldn't have been more wrong about his sexuality, incidentally. I think the only reason he never married is he was spoiled for choice.'

Benny hired him on a regular basis soon after and he was in the show, with a few gaps, until the end, moving on from singing to playing the young leading man role. Even when he got a bit too old to fit the description, Benny kept him, just insisting that the first thing Keefe did on arriving on the set every day was have the grey in his hair subtly darkened.

It was not all smooth sailing. Sometimes Benny would drop one of 'the family' briefly without explanation. It was not done to whinge or ask why. He didn't like that. Jon Jon Keefe was dropped at one point. He didn't realize it until he looked at the TV one night and saw 'The Benny Hill Show' with someone else playing his usual role of the barman or the waiter or the cuckolded husband. The following year, he got a call from Dennis Kirkland to come back. 'I asked him, "Was it something I said?" He said, "Oh don't piss about. Just get here. And don't make waves." And that was it. Nothing was ever mentioned again.'

An even earlier member of the team was Jenny Lee-Wright who had started her career as a dancer with Lionel Blair, but then been discovered by virtually every top comedian on British TV. Benny probably first spotted her when she was working with Morecambe and Wise. She was his ideal: blonde, glamorous, able to bring conviction to the silliest of sketches and with an excellent sense of comic timing.

The first time she appeared on the show she had only a tiny part. 'But he came round and spoke to us all and got to know us and made us feel at home. Lots of people I've worked with didn't bother to say hello to the lowest of the low, or even to the highest of the high! But it was very important to Benny to make us feel like a team. We were his own repertory company. I learned a lot from him. He would say, "Look, little heart, you are just not getting it right" and explain it till you did get it right. He couldn't stand fools. There were girls who were picked out during various shows and given a line or two, and if they were no good, they didn't come back. It was as simple as that. He gave advice to all the girls but a lot of them thought he was totally nutty, and went off and listened to their boyfriends instead. But he tried to give everyone at least one chance.'

Benny tended to keep the same leading ladies and character men for many years, but he changed his character actresses around more. He used Patricia Hayes, Rita Webb and several others over the years. One who eventually became a big favourite with him and stayed for many shows was Bella Emberg, later to serve another comic well as Blunderwoman to Russ Abbot's Cooperman. Bella was first booked to work with Benny on the very same show on which he first spotted Jackie Wright, at the BBC's Ealing Studios.

Bella recalled hearing Ben say that he'd wanted Rita Webb but her agent asked for too much money. It was probably one of Ben's jokes, but Bella, who was greatly in awe of him at that time, took it seriously. She had tried for twenty years to be a serious actress and went back to rep after working with Benny on that one occasion. But later she realized where her destiny lay, and returned to play the 'plain woman' who was the butt of so many of Benny's jokes. Benny's character would be chasing after one of the beautiful young girls and the punchline would be him ending up with Bella instead. It never bothered her that so many of the gags were at her expense. 'Benny was such a gentleman, he treated all the women in the show in exactly the same way, so you couldn't be offended by anything he asked you to do. He was nothing like the lecherous characters he played. He was the perfect gent.'

Bella loved to sit at rehearsals and watch Benny's methods of work. 'He taught me my comedy,' she said. 'With anyone else, I might get a script and not understand it so I'd have to say, "This doesn't feel quite right. What does this move mean, and why am I doing that?" But with Benny I just did it without question because I trusted him. And I knew that when I saw the finished result, I would understand precisely what he had been getting at. You never had to alter a word because every syllable was there for a reason. He understood his own business inside out. I don't think the world realizes yet that it has lost a genius who ranks alongside Charlie Chaplin and Stan Laurel.'

One of Benny's favourites was beautiful dark-eyed Louise English, whom he first spotted as a sixteen-year-old dancer with Pan's People. He asked her politely: 'May

I get in touch because I'm looking for girls for my show –
Goldie Hawn types who can sing and dance, and act in
sketches as well?'

Louise went into rep instead, but he rang about a year
later and asked her to be in the show. 'He was so charming
and polite, I said yes.' She had one line that first time. In
others, he wrote so much specially for her, he used to
tease her that it was becoming 'The Louise English Show'.

'It feels as if I knew him most of my life,' she says now.
Louise had been brought up by her mother alone, and
Benny became a substitute father-figure. 'He really was
like a father,' she told me. 'He was the first person I would
turn to for help and advice.' He adored her and thought
she was very talented. He advised her on work and lect-
ured her about smoking. He was very touched by her
closeness to her mother and urged her never to let go of
it. It reminded him of his relationship with his own
mother, he said.

When the time came for the fledgeling to fly the nest,
he did not try to stop her. It was just an unspoken understanding that she was ready to move on to other things.
From then on, he went to see every show, play or musical
she appeared in. 'I think he really was quite proud of me,'
she said.

His other favourite, of course, was Sue Upton, the pert
little blonde who had also joined the show when she was
very young. Benny spotted her photograph in a pile sent
to him by various agents. There was a special twinkle in
her eyes which made her stand out from the rest, he
thought, and he invited her along to Queensgate for an
audition.

Something about her total lack of pretention really
appealed to him. Most importantly she made him laugh.
Not only was she in every show, she was soon promoted

to be his most regular leading lady playing everything from glamorous saloon girls to his intrepid old lady, Wondergran.

Like Louise she regarded him as a father-figure. 'My father died when I was three. If someone wants to step into that place, you jump at the chance,' she said. 'He was there to help and protect me. I felt safe with him.'

11

The Fun Years

When 'The Benny Hill Show' arrived to film on location, it was as if the circus had come to town. The cast and crew would sometimes be one hundred strong. Filming dozens of different sketches and set-ups meant a very tight and complicated schedule. Two women, floor manager Fizz Waters and stage manager Auriol Lee, were the backbone of the outfit, and did an impressive job.

Benny frequently played several roles in one sketch, which meant a lot of time was spent waiting for him to get changed and made-up for each character. He had his own make-up caravan, but everyone else had to queue at the second which was often irksome. Complicated special effects set-ups also led to more standing around.

To crown it all the show was plagued with bad weather year after year. It always rained when they were on location and often the schedule was subject to last-minute changes which meant a lot of reorganization in which the dictates of the weather took precedence over the comfort of the cast.

Henry McGee is such a gentleman he is never heard to swear. 'Bother!' is about as far as he goes. But Bob Todd recalled one day when Henry was driven to the end of his tether. 'He was dressed as a ballerina. He got ready first, and as he left the caravan it was beginning to sleet.

He vanished into a mist in a little tutu, clutching a wand. But a few minutes later he was back.'

They weren't doing the ballerina sketch now, because of the weather, he reported. They were doing the one where he was a Russian general. He got changed into his Russian general costume, complete with boots and fur mittens. Off he went again. 'Five minutes later he was back. The sun had come out. They weren't doing the Russian sketch. He said I was the ballerina this time. He was a native shopkeeper.'

Henry got changed again and went into make-up to have a 'bone' put into his nose. Ballerina Bob started off for the set. 'No,' said Benny when he arrived. 'That's wrong. Henry should be the ballerina, Toddy. You're the aborigine.'

Toddy reported back to the caravan. It was the last straw. 'Henry went into the corner and screamed, "F***, f***, f***!" at the wall. Then he apologized profusely.'

Sometimes the weather was so bad, they could do nothing and just had to sit it out. But it was important that people didn't get bored and depressed during the waits. Dispirited actors do not make for good comedy sketches. So the order of the day was fun, fun, fun.

'The family' all looked forward to it every year. They were excited to see one another again, and swap stories of what they had been doing since the last batch of shows. And they knew that there were plenty of laughs in store, off screen as well as on.

They always had to be within a few miles of Thames' studios because of union regulations about travelling time. But Bob Todd found it too difficult to get backwards and forwards every day from his home in a remote East Sussex village. So he would move into a room in a local pub for the duration of the shoot – anything up to three weeks – and every morning Kirkland would pick him up and drive him to the set. 'One year, one of the pubs refused to take him because they didn't want the aggravation of having the film people in,' recalled Jon Jon Keefe. 'So they got him a room at the pub across the way which was going bankrupt. At lunchtime people would be in that pub, because it was Toddy's pub, at the end of the day the whole crew would be there and at the end of filming we had a party in the back garden. After three weeks, a pub which had been nearly broke could practically pay off its mortgage. The guvnor at the first pub was kicking himself.'

Not that Benny himself went into the pubs. Every lunchtime he retired to his caravan for a light salad and a quick catnap, or else spent the time making notes on new ideas. When Dennis went to call him for the afternoon session, Benny would hand over a list of extra props and effects he needed and say: 'I don't suppose there's any chance of having these, little heart?' At the end of the day, after a chat with Kirkland about the next morning's requirements, he would be driven straight home.

Benny didn't really approve of the drinking. He wanted everyone to take the filming as seriously and care about it as much as he did. So after lunch the reprobates would return to the set frantically sucking peppermints and spraying Gold Spot into their mouths. 'We wafted in on a cloud of Polo mint,' said Keefe. 'We had a theory that Toddy was having Gold Spot specially made up with a vodka base because one squirt from his bottle would knock you backwards.'

Nor did Benny join in any of the bad language which was often used on the set. No one can remember ever hearing him use a profanity. 'But Kirkland would be saying and doing the most outrageous things, and you'd hear this tremulous little snigger from where Benny was sitting,' said Jon Jon Keefe.

When he was on camera, Benny often laughed at all the wrong moments. He was a tremendous giggler. 'We had wonderful laughing sessions,' said Bob Todd. 'I remember once we were doing a "Bonanza" send-up. He was dressed as Hoss and I was a Red Indian, with one feather. We ended up doing thirty-two takes! Benny was on a platform to make him look big. I held a map, and all I had to do was point once and say "White man's country", point again and say, "Red man's country". Benny took one look at me and said, "No, no, I can't." He was hysterical every time I spoke. The director was going mad, people were screaming. Thirty-two takes altogether.'

Toddy also recalled an American Civil War sketch which set Benny off in hysterics. Benny was Massa Gaylord come back to claim his bride. He also played the bride, Miss Abigail, while Toddy was a black servant. As soon as Benny heard Toddy's Southern accent and saw his flat-footed walk flapping across the set, his shoulders started to shake. Each attempt at a take made him shake more and more with suppressed laughter. 'His shoulders and cheeks were a blur,' recalled Toddy proudly. 'He couldn't speak.'

The sketch, however, did not amuse the Americans so much when it was shown in the States in 1976 during a special promotional week of Thames' programmes on a New York station. Toddy's black make-up and exaggerated portrayal offended the racially sensitive audience. It was one of the factors which made Thames realize they would need to rethink and re-edit the shows if they were ever to sell them in America.

The laughs continued back at the studio on the days

they recorded there without an audience. Toddy was a high court judge on one occasion, with Benny and the rest of the cast as the jury. 'I did my judge's voice, "Ladies and gentlemen of the jury, it is up to you to decide whether this book will corrupt or deprave." I looked down in the jury box and Benny had his head down because he was laughing so much. We cut and started again. "Ladies and gentlemen of the jury ..." He got the giggles again. He was biting his tongue not to laugh. Eventually after several attempts, he said, "OK Den, I'm all right now." I said "Ladies and gentlemen of the jury", and Jenny Lee-Wright suddenly started shrieking. They tried to hide me from their view with scenery. In the end, they cleared them out of the studio and put them out in the corridor while I did the lines. We just couldn't carry on.'

Dennis once told Toddy: 'Benny will never do a show without you. But you'd be amazed how many times he has to rewrite your lines because he knows there are certain words you couldn't say without setting him off.' And Benny's giggling never let up in twenty years.

The laughs little Jackie Wright used to get on screen paled dramatically beside the ones he raised when they were filming. He could never get anything right. People would gather round just to watch him get it wrong time and time again. He was famous for forgetting lines. 'As a line-forgetter they could put medals on me,' he once told me ruefully. 'Sometimes I have to do a scene quite a few times, and Benny begins to get a bit irritated with me. Lately they don't even show me the script! They don't let me know what's going on, they just tell me what I have to say immediately before I say it.' If he managed to say it.

But even in a silent sketch without a line to remember, he would make a hash of it. There was once a quickie where they were all at the Opticians Ball. When the toast-master gave the toast, they were each supposed to put their glass to their right eye like an eye bath. Jackie put his to his lips and solemnly drank it.

He ate non-stop. He would have an apple in one hand, a cigarette in the other, a packet of crisps in his pocket, and spray biscuit crumbs as he spoke. After Benny's birthday party lunches, Jackie took the leftovers home for his tea.

Benny liked all 'the family' and the girls to be there for the whole duration of the filming. It was not done to ask for a few days' off for other jobs. You were either available for the full three weeks or not at all. One year Jon Jon Keefe discovered after he'd been booked that the filming was starting a week earlier than he'd anticipated. He was already commited to another job so he turned up for Benny's show a couple of days late.

'I arrived at the location in Leatherhead and the first thing Kirkland said to me was, "Put a wig on, put a dress on, put a cardy on and some high heels." ' Keefe suspected a joke but looked round and saw that Toddy was similarly clad. 'Kirkland insisted the first sketch was wig, dress, cardy, shoes. So I went to wardrobe and make-up. Wig, dress, cardy, high heels. Full slap make-up. Then we get in the bus and go to somebody's back garden in Ashtead, and it was a glorious day, ninety degrees, and I'm sitting around all morning in wig, dress, cardy, etc.' By lunch-time, he still hadn't been called.

'Kirkland told me to get down to the pub. I said, "Like this?" He said they'd already been there a couple of days and all the locals were used to actors in costume, so I went to the pub.' By this time, his stubble was beginning to show through the make-up. 'There were all these old codgers sitting round this pub and I walked up to the bar and said, "A pint of lager for me and one for my friend," and they all stared at me as if I was from outer space. Wig, dress, cardy, high heels, stubble. Every finger in the village was pointing at me. When we got back to the site I was so fed up, I took it all off but Kirkland made me put it straight back on again. Fresh make-up.' At 5.15, he started to take it all off once more. Kirkland strolled over, with Benny watching intently, trying to keep his face straight. 'Just what do you think you are doing? I know I'm only the director on this show and you obviously think you are the star, but put it back on again.'

By this time, Keefe was nearly in tears. Minutes later, Kirkland finally said: 'I've just been talking to Benny and this is obviously rather delicate, but he would like to know why you've been dressed as a woman all day.' The whole sixty-strong crew, in on the joke, applauded as he added: 'DON'T BE LATE FOR FILMING AGAIN!' And Benny piped up: 'Yes, dear heart, he's right. Don't be late again.'

The jokes were mostly real boys' stuff. The girls would all sit around knitting and talking about their boyfriends. The men took them so much for granted they ignored them.

Jon Jon Keefe remembered one day when they were rehearsing at a sports club. A coach pulled up and a coachload of teenage girls in skimpy navy hockey outfits got out and walked towards the hockey pitch. 'Every guy in that room rushed over to the window going "Cor, look at that!" And the driver and his mate were looking in our window, at our girls in their leotards, and doing exactly the same thing! But we never took any notice of the Angels.'

Sometimes, though, it was difficult not to take notice of Sue Upton when Benny wrote in all sorts of stunts for her to do, either as Wondergran or some other character.

Especially when her bosom blew up. One day she was WonderGirl being chased round by the baddies. The gag was that she turned round, whipped open her cape and fired at them with machine-guns concealed in her bra. 'I was all wired up so I expected a few bangs,' she said, 'but when they came they were not so much bangs as minor explosions. I thought I was about to lose part of my vital equipment.'

One of Benny's favourite days every year was his birthday, which generally fell during rehearsals. The girls all brought him presents, and a crate of wine or champagne would be hidden somewhere in the rehearsal room. From mid-morning it was champagne all the way, and little work got done. In later years, he developed a tradition of taking the whole cast and crew out to lunch.

It was Jon Jon Keefe's birthday on the same day. 'I'd get in early and there would be a tiny little cake for me tucked away in a cupboard in the corner. So they'd celebrate my birthday and get the little one out of the way, then Kirkland would say, "Right, let's go and do the big one." '

Even after Philip Jones had retired from Thames, Benny would invite him to join them. He wrote to Philip in January 1989: 'You are cordially invited, which means you will only drink cordial. We meet about 11–11.30 at the rehearsal room and go on to a restaurant later.' It was Benny's last birthday lunch with the cast.

Even though they all had such fun together, Benny would be under enormous pressure by the time they got through all the filming and the studio inserts. Then he had to face the part he hated most, the night the audience came in. For him, the laughter stopped at this point.

He cut his contact with the audience down to a minimum. He would come on and do a warm-up routine with Dennis Kirkland, then he might do one song or recitation. The audience watched most of the rest of the show on monitors, adding a laughter track to stuff that had already been recorded. But even this frightened Benny. When he went on to do the warm-up he carried a very heavy book, a trick to stop his hands from shaking. 'Oh, why do we put ourselves through it?' he'd moan.

'What people didn't see was him standing backstage sweating more than I thought it was possible to sweat,' said Jon Jon Keefe. 'The last thing I would say to him as I passed him in the corridor coming from make-up was, "They're on your side, you know." He'd say, "I know but it doesn't make it any easier." On studio days his voice would go to a croak from the pressure.'

Bob Todd said that audience night was the only time he ever saw Benny's personality change at all. 'Other times, he was always the same, in twenty years he never had a bad mood. The only time he was different, and you had to be a bit careful, was when the audience was in. Otherwise – and this is quite hard to explain – he would be the same on the first Monday morning as at the end of the filming. His demeanour never changed. He'd come in exactly the same every day. "Morning Toddy, morning Henry", always the same. And he always left in just the same mood to go back to an empty house. You never got the impression of any variation in his life at all.'

12

Spreading His Wings

Benny began 1984 by celebrating his sixtieth birthday –
whether he liked it or not! For many years, he pretended
he was born in 1925, giving that date in various reference
books. People who thought the real date was a year earlier
and queried it, would get an enigmatic reply. 'Maybe I
decided to be a year younger,' he would say, 'or maybe I
didn't.'

Thames wanted to give him a proper sixtieth birthday
party, so associate producer Nigel Cook was given the job
of checking Benny's true age, and enlisted my help. We
worked out he really had been born in 1924, so Nigel
bought a piece of silver at Aspreys and had it suitably
engraved. At the presentation Benny was rather taken
aback that his fib had been rumbled, but accepted it with
good grace.

It was the start of an adventurous year for him. Ever
since his shows had been screened in America, there had
been constant requests for him to go over there. He was
asked to fly out simply to promote the show, or to guest
on other TV shows, or to appear in cabaret. Not knowing
of Benny's fear of live audiences, the Americans had no
idea that all the millions of dollars in Las Vegas would
not have persuaded him to appear.

Sometimes the Americans decided his imminent

capitulation was a fait accompli, and stories appeared in the press announcing that he was about to star in one gambling centre or another. Benny's press cuttings service, which now covered the whole world, would duly turn these reports up and he would fume with indignation over their inaccuracy.

'There's one story here that I am going to appear in cabaret in Atlantic City, which I didn't know anything about until I read it!' he told me one day. 'It says the whole cast is going out there with me. At rehearsals the other day they all kept asking me when we were off. And little Jackie is terrified. He keeps saying, "I'm not going over there, I want to go home to Belfast." '

The one thing that might have tempted Benny over to the States was the one thing he was not offered. He liked doing commercials, and these had been the excuse for many of the European and Australian jaunts in the past. He did commercials in Australia specifically so that he could go and see his sister Diana – at someone else's expense. But the Americans assumed he'd want the big money Vegas could offer.

The thought of performing in Las Vegas left him cold. 'They have been writing to me for years and there's an awful lot of money on offer,' he said. 'I understand that business is not that good over there, the people who top the bills are the same ones who've topped for years. I mean it must be lovely to see Tom Jones or Sammy Davis, but not if you saw them last year and the year before. So these people write to me and say they are looking for a new attraction and I would be it!' He turned them straight down. 'I answer all the letters, "Dear sir, thank you for your kind letter ...", and then I throw them away.'

Sometimes the casino bosses would suggest he went over first as their guest, took a friend, stayed as long as he liked, acclimatized himself, saw what sort of material worked in Vegas, and then thought again. They didn't realize the main drawback. Benny neither needed nor wanted the money. 'It's a terrible thing to admit in these days of recession, but I don't need to work. I just work for pleasure. I don't work for harassment and aggro, however much money is involved.' He also claimed to be troubled by the thought that there might be one night when the Vegas bosses were in the audience, and he wasn't very good. 'And bang would go my knee-caps.'

In 1984, though, his curiosity about the States got the better of him. He decided to go incognito for a short holiday, just to get the feel of the place, but still wasn't confident enough to go alone. He asked Dennis Kirkland if he would like to keep him company.

When Dennis duly asked Thames if he could take some of his holiday and told them where he was going, Philip Jones was horrified that Benny was just going to make his own way and his own arrangements. On his first trip to the States, he needed to be treated like a star. So Thames took over the organization of the journey. It was arranged for Benny and Dennis to meet Don Taffner in New York, an ideal opportunity for Taffner to show his star off to just a few of the clients who were gratefully buying every 'Benny Hill Show' they could get hold of.

First the pair went to San Francisco and Los Angeles. The news of the trip had leaked out by then, and they were met in San Francisco by a reporter and photographer from Britain's *Daily Star*, who had kindly brought along their own pretty model for Benny to be pictured with.

In an imaginative piece of writing in next day's *Star*, the girl claimed: 'As we walked the streets hand in hand, cuddled over lunch and spent a romantic day and evening, I saw the real Benny Hill. He's a very loving and affectionate man.' To Benny, alas, she was just another photo opportunity and he forgot her existence when he described his trip afterwards. He always maintained he had met no girls at all the whole time they were there.

In Los Angeles they had hung around the hotel pool all day, even having their meals there, waiting for some typical starlets to turn up. Wasn't that how everyone in Hollywood spent their time? But the only person they saw all day was Bruce Forsyth.

Optimistically, Benny went to a party at Hugh Heffner's Playboy mansion. After greeting Benny, the pyjama-clad Hef went off to bed and told everyone to stay and enjoy themselves, but Benny found the atmosphere strangely virginal. Another legend bit the dust.

A reception was organized for Benny at which he met Jack Lemmon and comedian Steve Allen. Clint Eastwood, another fervent fan, had set out from his home in Carmel to attend but his helicopter had been held up by bad weather. Burt Reynolds couldn't make it either, but sent an invitation to tea at his home instead. Surely Benny thought, they would meet some women there. Burt was a sex symbol after all.

When Benny and Dennis arrived, Burt picked up the phone and cooed happily to someone at the other end: 'He's here! Come on over!' 'I thought this must be it at last,' said Benny. 'I assumed he was summoning some girls. But it was a pal of his, the comedian Dom de Luise.'

The four men talked shop and laughed uproariously for a couple of hours, then Burt had to make a brief TV appearance on a talent show called 'Starsearch'. It was decided they would all accompany him and go out for dinner afterwards. Of course, Benny thought. That must be when the girls would be joining them. The restaurant was packed with typical film industry 'wannabees' and

Benny at his happiest, among the girls (*Scope Features*).

Benny Hill

01-584-6921

2 Queensgate
London
S.W.7

Feb 1 '86

Dear Philip,

"Ta" for your letter re "Last Words". Please do go ahead & use the little interview piece Dennis & I did.

I don't think I thank you for your kind Xmas present, the Port & Stilton. I took the cheese to a Cheese & Wine party in Chelsea, & I took the port to a Port & Puddin' party in Pimlico.

Hope you are well.

Yours,

B

Benny's letters to Philip Jones were always full of jokes (*Philip Jones*).

7, Fairwater House, Twickenham Rd.,
Teddington MIDDX
JAN 2 89.

"Dear Philp"!!!

This year, Ben's Birthday Lunch is on 20TH JAN. You are cordially invited. Which means you will only drink cordial!

We meet about 11 → 11.30 AM at rehearsal room :-
The Charlton Hotel, The Green,
Hampton Court, SURREY
& go on to a restaurant later.

Please let Dennis or me know if you can make it.

Look forward to seeing you soon.

Take care.

Yours,

Benny.

'hasbeens'. But no girls came to join them. Benny's illusions about life in the movie capital were shattered once again.

He was quietly thrilled about the people he *did* meet. 'Fancy,' he told me, 'I used to go and see all Mickey Rooney's films when I was a kid, and think he was wonderful, and now here he is saying he's a fan of mine. I can hardly believe it.'

In New York, Don Taffner, who owned a restaurant as well as his TV business at the time, threw a small party which enabled him to show off both the restaurant and Benny. He figured that Benny might pretend to be reluctant about such events, but like most 'pieces of talent', he would be offended if such a party wasn't on offer. He guessed correctly. Benny was beginning to enjoy the Americans' uninhibited welcome and the way people would just come up to him in the street and tell him they loved him.

Another night they went to a Mexican restaurant to indulge Benny's love of Spanish-style food and music. He also attended a boxing match. But he spent three of his New York evenings at Don and Eleanor's house just watching TV.

The whole trip was a success. And it gave him a taste for travelling as a star, instead of his usual anonymous wanderings.

Benny had been entered for the Golden Rose of Montreux TV festival on several occasions, but never bothered to attend when he was merely another competitor. The Swiss festival's definition of Light Entertainment encompassed everything from ice skating to game shows, but in 1984 Benny had been awarded the City of Montreux's special prize for the funniest show. The 'Rose' was picked up by Dennis Kirkland.

In 1985, Benny was invited to attend the twenty-fifth anniversary festival of the Golden Rose to receive a special award. It was for any winner from any previous year whose programme had subsequently been seen in more countries than any other. Obviously dreamed up just to get their most famous competitor there, he agreed to accept it in person.

Eighteen months before, Benny had been in the Cromwell Hospital with a bleeding ulcer. He was amazed at the fuss the press made. When he had a kidney removed because of a non-malignant growth in 1978, nobody noticed, he complained. But now he was headline news.

I called round to see him the day after he came out of hospital. He'd said on the phone that I'd have to have black coffee as he didn't have any milk or tea in, so I took some with me. I bought a pile of morning papers, a pint of milk, and for some reason that now escapes me, took four tea bags out of a packet I had at home. He was astounded. 'I thought I was the one who was supposed to be mean,' he teased. 'Couldn't you manage five?' I offered to do some proper shopping for him, but he insisted he was well enough to go and do it himself. I think he was afraid I'd come back with three potatoes, six cornflakes and two ounces of sugar.

He was in a good mood, convinced that the ulcer had healed. He kept raving about the gold taps in the Cromwell bathrooms, did jokes about the cold bedpans, and described how Louise and Sue had joined him for a meal in his room. He said the doctor had told him to limit himself to half a bottle of wine with meals, so he was planning to have twelve meals a day.

However, the ulcer troubled him for years afterwards whenever he was worried, and he was worried when he got to Montreux. He was pale and sweating with pain. At that time there was a pop festival run in conjunction with the TV contest. All the top groups would jet in, mime to their latest record and jet hastily out again. The hotel where Benny was staying was under siege by hundreds of expensively dressed teenage girls from all the surrounding Swiss finishing schools, looking for their pop idols. Benny barricaded himself in his room. Several of the girls asked what his room number was, but he was not even in the mood for a visit.

Worse still, he had forgotten the pills for the pain from his ulcer. He looked dreadful. But someone arranged for his doctor to phone a local pharmacy and tell them what his prescription was and eventually he decided he felt well enough to come up the mountain and have some photographs taken. It was a bizarre outing.

Halfway up we stopped at a restaurant for lunch. The proprietor of the Restaurant de la Gare, Helmut Emele, recognized his new client, fetched a trumpet and serenaded us with a shrill rendition of *Oh Mein Papa*. The photographers wanted pictures against the exquisite mountain backdrop. Benny wouldn't do it without a girl in the shot. So a young waitress was commandeered from Helmut to be Benny's latest photo opportunity.

By the time we got to the top, there was deep snow and poor light. Benny and I shivered in a café for half an hour while the photographers built a snowman as a prop. Then he did a hasty Fred Scuttle salute to oblige them before his fingers went numb with the cold.

It all ended happily. The cabaret at the awards ceremony included a Russian mime artist whose act went on far too long for most of us, but for Benny made the whole trip to Switzerland worth while.

Eric Morecambe, one of Britain's best-loved comedians

and a fellow Thames artist, died in 1984. A few months later, Thames decided to mount a huge tribute to him, a gala concert at the London Palladium to be recorded for later transmission on TV.

In the past, Philip Jones had occasionally asked Benny if he would appear on some Thames variety show which needed a 'top of the bill'. Benny had always said no. He repeated his theory that any appearances outside his show frittered away the coinage and made him less of an event. Now, as an important part of the Thames stable, Benny was invited to appear on Eric's show. It was to be recorded in front of a huge audience and so it seemed likely he would refuse as usual. He hadn't been on a stage for nearly twenty-five years, but his feelings for Eric made him say yes.

Despite a terrible attack of nerves, Benny got through it. He did his schoolmaster act, reading from a large heavy book, which once again helped prevent his hands from shaking. Afterwards Prince Philip chatted to him and said: 'I hear this is your first appearance on stage for twenty-odd years. You must have been a child star.' Benny was very chuffed. And he loved Mike Yarwood's response when Jimmy Tarbuck also marvelled that Benny hadn't set foot on a stage for a quarter of a century. 'He ought to get himself a better agent!'

After this success, Thames felt confident enough to ask Benny to make a second stage appearance, this time before a particularly demanding audience. In March 1987, the American television industry was honouring Thames Television with a special 'Salute to Thames' week. As part of this, the company was invited to put on a live show featuring some of its artists at the Lincoln Center on Broadway, to be followed by a gala dinner at the Plaza Hotel. Who better to top the bill than the comedian whose shows had become synonymous with British TV for most American viewers? The question was whether Benny could be persuaded to do it. The 2,000-strong audience would largely consist of executives of the TV industry. About as tough and critical a crowd as you could get. Benny agreed to do it. Philip Jones said: 'I think he did it partly as a favour for me, and partly because he knew he would be flying the flag for the company. But it was done in fear and trepidation. This was really pushing the boat out for Benny.' I was in the party when Benny flew to New York, on 24 March. Also in the group were Mike Yarwood and Suzanne Danielle, who were to portray Prince Charles and Princess Diana, Janet Brown, who would appear as Margaret Thatcher, singers Chas and Dave and lyricist Richard Stilgoe. Henry McGee and some of the Angels accompanied Benny. Edward Woodward was to join us in New York.

The trip did not start well. The plane we were due to catch from Gatwick went out of service and they did not have another to replace it. We sat around for most of the day. No one from British Caledonian's public relations department came to apologize, despite the starry cast in the VIP lounge. Some of the party got drunk. Others wanted to go home. But Benny was calm, unruffled and uncomplaining. Melanie Louis, from Thames' press office, kept apologizing to him for the delay, but he was as good as gold. He said: 'It's not your fault, little heart.' And at least the long wait allowed one of the Angels to change her outfit about three times, to everyone else's amusement. Eventually we all had to transfer to Heathrow and get a flight from there instead.

When Benny arrived at Kennedy Airport in the small hours, it caused chaos. The lengthy queues waiting to go through the usual entry formalities stood in amazement as immigration and customs officials left their posts and leaped over luggage belts to greet him. Benny, meanwhile, was trying to take his own baggage off the carousel. He seriously did not expect anyone to do it for him.

On the following day, after a morning's rehearsal, we all went up the Empire State Building. Once again, Benny drew crowds. They stopped looking at the view and looked at Benny instead, who obliged with a few Fred Scuttle salutes. Mike Yarwood joked: 'Why have I come all these thousands of miles just to watch Benny Hill signing autographs?'

Benny's nerves about the show were lessened by the fact that Henry McGee was to be in the first sketch with him. 'Henry'll get me through,' he said. And he did. Benny sidled on stage as Fred Scuttle with his back to the audience and then turned round and leered, blinking at the massive audience. They roared.

At the banquet afterwards, Benny was seated with the Taffners, Dennis Kirkland, Sue Upton and Henry. He wanted people that he knew round him, to provide his usual barrier against the outside world. But even he had to admit that he was moved by the sheer boisterousness of the Americans' adulation. He was the hero of the hour.

Next day he treated some of us to lunch at an open air restaurant on the river. Then we went shopping to look for toys for Sue Upton's children. Sue and I got very giggly about the size of the stretch limo put at Benny's disposal, but he took to it as to the manner born. He was beginning to enjoy America. He would go back several times over the next four years, nearly always to awards ceremonies and other big functions – the very things that he avoided assiduously at home. The Americans' uncomplicated enthusiasm for his work, and the absence of snide comments about his lifestyle, boosted his morale enormously at a time when Britain seemed to be turning against him.

13

Homeless Again

In 1986, the twenty-five-year lease on Benny's flat in Queensgate expired and he decided not to renew it. He had fallen out of love with the place after the owners started building work to add an extra storey to the top of the block. The whole place had been shrouded in scaffolding and tarpaulin for almost two years. It was ruining the quality of Benny's life. Apart from the inconvenience of having reduced light and not being able to use his balcony, it offended his increasing obsession with privacy to have workmen clambering past the windows. 'What if I've got a girl in there?' he said. 'Every time I look up I see a workman looking back at me. I've had to have the blinds drawn for months now, there are tins of paint and mess everywhere, it's misery.'

Another consideration, obviously, was money. The area had become popular with the oil sheikhs, and prices had risen accordingly. The owners now wanted to charge about £500,000 for the new lease. Of course Benny had the money, but his irritation with the building work tipped the balance and he decided to get out. The problem was he had nowhere to go.

He looked rather half-heartedly at some other flats, then thought of buying a house, then couldn't decide where to buy one. 'I had hoped to find somewhere before

I had to leave Queensgate, and I looked at a place near Richmond, but it just wasn't right,' he said. 'I don't really know what I want. If it's too big I've got to have someone to live in and look after it. And if you have a housekeeper, you might as well get married and have a family, and I'm not going to do that now.'

He had also got worried about the number of stories about celebrities sold to the tabloids by people in their employ. 'If I had a house it would be sure to have a garden, and then I'd have to have a gardener who might give stories about me to the papers,' he said anxiously. From that point on, he never even had a regular cleaner. He just used a cleaning agency who sent two different women each time, so that he didn't get to know them and they couldn't get to know him.

The housing dilemma continued to preoccupy him for the next six years. He decided on a temporary solution. He would go and live in the semi his mother had left him, the old family home in Westrow Gardens, Southampton. After all, there must have been a reason she had made him promise never to sell it. It was always meant to be a stop-gap. Benny didn't even take his furniture. In June 1986, he put it all, including *TV Times'* famous plush chesterfields, into storage at Pickfords. It was still there when he died.

All he took with him was a few personal belongings and his papers. Sue Upton's husband Roger Whatling came round to drive him to his new home. 'He had to put a trailer on the back of the car as well as a roof-rack,' Benny told me. 'Fancy me having enough bits and pieces to fill a roof-rack, because I'm not a possessions person at all.' That was after a mere twenty-five years in one place!

He insisted that he felt no sadness at leaving the flat.

The misery of the building works had wiped out any sentiment.

Once he moved to Southampton, he loved it. Westrow Gardens is beautifully placed between Southampton football club and the county cricket ground, and a few yards from the rural charms of Southampton Common. No. 22 is a solidly-built semi-detached house of the kind so common in the thirties, quite large as such houses go, and in good condition. It certainly wasn't 'shabby' or 'crumbling' as it was later to be described. It has a wrought-iron gate and a tiny garden at the front. Benny told Dennis Kirkland he had spent a fortune on rose trees for it, but it is only big enough to hold a dozen!

There is a small garden at the back too, invisible from the road, where Benny could sit outside and work on his writing. The house was still furnished with his mother's furniture and Benny saw no reason to change it. Some said he deliberately kept it as a shrine to her, but I think it was probably more likely that he simply had no interest in interior decoration or furnishings, and could not be bothered to go to a lot of unnecessary trouble when no one was going to see it. Especially as it was, after all, only temporary.

Because he did not intend to stay there long, he didn't bother to have any personal stationery printed as he had at Queensgate. He started writing letters on cheap lined notepaper that he bought at Woolworth's because he couldn't really see the difference between that and expensive unlined quality vellum. He once tried to do me some good by writing to my editor praising the accuracy of a feature I had done about him, but because it was on such a scrappy little piece of lined paper, I don't think my boss really believed it could be from Benny Hill.

At first, he was uneasy about people knowing where

he was living. I don't think he was ashamed of it. He just had a faint sense that it wasn't quite suitable for a man of his stature. And it was terribly accessible to the public. There was no security, no lock on the gate, and the front door was only a few feet from the road. For some reason, he was listed in the Southampton phone book, under A.H. Hill. He hadn't even bothered to be ex-directory. So he tried for a while to conceal his exact whereabouts. He asked me to state in print that he was 'staying with friends in the Southampton area'.

The whole business disorientated him. He did no shows that year, the first gap in his record with Thames. When they later sacked him and pretended he had just decided to take a break, they used this example to prove that Benny had, in fact, taken time off before.

Until he had moved, he could not settle to do any writing. And once he was in Southampton, he began a new love affair with the county of his childhood. 'I've got very lazy,' he said. 'Being down there so near to the Isle of Wight and the New Forest, I just can't do any writing at all.' He'd take a ferry from Southampton either to the Isle of Wight or across to the Forest area and then just walk for miles. 'There's one lovely pub in the New Forest called the Travellers' Rest that I go to a lot,' he told me. 'I love sitting outside with a beer. It's a three-mile walk from the ferry to the pub and back again, but that's no problem because I can easily do twenty miles a day. I walk and walk, and don't even notice I'm walking, just like I do in the Camargue when I'm in France. A reporter from a local paper was so surprised just to see me trotting along the other day, he ran up and asked me if I'd retired. But it's not even semi-retirement. And I think most of the locals know I was born in Southampton so they're not too surprised to see me ambling around.'

He now thought he might buy a pied-à-terre in London and a larger house in Hampshire. He told one friend he was looking for a house in either the New Forest or the Isle of Wight. The trouble was, he said, that he could not find anything expensive enough. His accountant had told him he must spend about a million pounds. The idea of Benny coping with the responsibilities of owning a mansion was ludicrous.

The fact was that Westrow Gardens suited him. It may have been small, but it was big enough for a bachelor with few personal possessions and no interest in acquiring any more. It was humble, but he didn't care because he was so unassuming himself. This modest little house became his haven. Very few people were allowed over the door-step. One or two of the neighbours who had been there since his mother's day would pop in and out, but new-comers were not really welcome.

He started seeing a lot more of his cousin Chris Hill, also still unmarried, and the pair went for long walks. 'We talked about everything under the sun,' Chris said. 'We were a couple of windbags, but Benny was worse than I was. He was one of the few people who could shut me up! That was when we were on our own, of course. If there were a lot of people about he was inclined to retreat into his shell. He'd be happier sat in the corner by him-self.'

Benny also looked up other old friends with whom he felt able to relax. He used to call on neighbour Mimi Levy, whose family had been friendly with the Hills since the thirties. She provided a link with his mother, and she spoiled him the way his mother had. She used to make his favourite cream meringues for him.

He discovered a new marina in Southampton called Ocean Village, full of restaurants and clubs, which he told me was almost as good as the South of France. And he was pleasantly surprised to find there were now topless sunbathers on the dear old Isle of Wight. 'But that's not the real attraction,' he added hastily. He also had some very old friends living on the island. He had originally got to know a husband and wife comedy act called Billy Whittaker and Mimi Law back in the fifties when they were all on the same bill at the Palace, Plymouth.

Benny had told them then: 'It's good to meet you at last. I've had you rammed down my throat for years!' It turned out Benny's parents were great fans of their act, and never missed them when they were appearing in Southampton. They used to tell the family's aspiring comedian: 'Go and see Billy and Mimi. You might learn something.'

The Whittakers came across Benny again a few years later when he was a big TV star, but still doing some live work. He was due to play the Wellington Pier, Great Yarmouth, but was rushed into hospital with appendicitis. Billy and Mimi stood in for him at short notice.

In the seventies, shortly after Benny had inherited Westrow Gardens from his mother, he heard that the Whittakers were in Ryde. Billy was entertainments officer for the Medina half of the island. One day the barman at the Ryde Pavilion told Mimi there was a fellow outside who said he knew them, but hadn't seen them for years. 'And do you know,' he added, 'he looks exactly like Benny Hill! They could be twins.' Benny greeted them: 'I've just come to say thank you properly for standing in for me that time.' Billy told him: 'You daft old fool, that was twenty years ago!' They had a wonderful day reminiscing about old times. Benny was drinking strong brown ale in those days, downing the stuff right left and centre, according to the Whittakers.

Now that he was actually living so close, he became a regular visitor to their home. He would turn up at very short notice, walking down the drive carrying two plastic bags clanking with bottles of champagne. He loved to sit and gossip about all the old acts they had known in variety. But when the others screamed with laughter about how bad some performer or other had been, Benny didn't join in. He still had his rule about never saying anything unkind about another artist.

One day at the Whittakers' house, he was re-acquainted with another old friend. Sylvia Thorley is an agent and entertainment consultant who had first met Benny in 1979 when she used to take dancers to audition for his show. She'd escort them to the flat in Queensgate first, and if they were booked for the show, she'd accompany them to the studio.

They would eventually become very close, but at first Sylvia didn't understand how Benny hated to be crowded. Sometimes when she'd gone to the studio she'd taken him some little present and realized by his cool reception that she'd done the wrong thing. Now she invited him to come to visit her and her husband Brian at their home in Bonchurch, a still quaintly Victorian village in the southern part of the island.

He immediately said no. Then one day she heard that he had been seen walking around the area, obviously checking the place out. Shortly afterwards he rang to invite himself over. These island friendships were to stand Benny in good stead a few years later, when he found himself with far too much time on his hands.

Sylvia was one of the few people who was ever allowed into Westrow Gardens. She'd telephone to say she was passing through Southampton on her way back home from Torquay, so they met for lunch. Afterwards, Benny suddenly suggested they take a taxi back to his house, where they carried on drinking and watched the inevitable videos. She said: 'It was a perfectly ordinary house, the furniture may have been old-fashioned, but it certainly wasn't shabby the way it was described in the papers. I think people went overboard about it. It was just an ordinary little room we were in, with no fancy things around. I was flattered that he'd invited me.'

The Southampton idyll suddenly ended when Benny felt an overwhelming urge to get back to work. The good weather had broken, and as he said: 'Southampton in the rain isn't exactly Paris. I always intended to start work again before long.'

He wrote enough material to begin filming in the summer of 1987. His accommodation problems still preoccupied him. Dennis Kirkland's wife, Mary, or Sue Upton would get details of houses from estate agents and check them out to see if they were remotely suitable. Benny always had some objection. They were too near a church, the neighbours had a dog, they were too big, too small, there was too much garden or not enough garden.

In the end Dennis found a furnished flat in Fairwater House, a stone's throw from Thames' studio. Benny took it, paying a year's rent in advance, without even bothering to look at it properly. He moved in with his most precious possessions, his two TV sets, his video and a vast stock of tapes.

The other residents respected his increasing need for privacy, but Benny always contributed the biggest bottle of champagne to any get-togethers the residents' association organized, like the Bonfire Night party.

In the past, he had often travelled to Teddington from Queensgate by train. Other big Thames stars would drive past him in their Rolls Royces as he walked from the station with his script in a carrier bag. This was the man responsible for the financial success of the station, and for some of them having Rolls Royces. Now he could walk happily to work in two minutes without anyone laughing at him. No one could expect him to take a limo for a journey of one third of a mile.

Some newspapers, fed up with waiting for him to buy the home they felt he deserved, started printing reports that he had bought villas in Spain or apartments in the South of France. As usual, he was exasperated by the inaccuracies. I'd ring him up and he'd say: 'I'm not here, how can I be here? I'm living in the South of France, don't you read the papers?' Then he'd add: 'I've just been looking at a nice penthouse on the river here. It was lovely but it wasn't quite what I want, so I think I'll carry on looking ...'

Now he repeated the same sort of love affair he'd been having with Hampshire, only this time it was with the river Thames between Richmond and Kingston. He became a familiar figure walking up and down the towpath on his way to the shopping centre in one or the other.

He liked all his journeys to have a purpose. 'I never go for a walk as such,' he said. 'Even in the New Forest, I gave myself the target of having lunch at the other end of the walk. I can't just walk for no reason. If I go along the river it's because I'm going from the flat to a particular shop in Richmond, or a good food shop in Kingston. I walk along the towpath and stop at a pub like the Three Pigeons on the way for a drink and a bite to eat, and I go to Smiths and get some papers. Then I go to Woollies or Marks and Spencer and get some really expensive clothes, before walking back on the other side of the river.' He meant this as a joke, but of course he really did shop at Woolworth's and Marks.

He also discovered restaurants he really enjoyed in the area. 'When I was at Queensgate, I was forever hopping into a car and going out to Skindles at Maidenhead or the Compleat Angler at Marlow, but I haven't been for ages because it's so nice round here. Mind you, I intend to go to the Roux Brothers' place at Bray, the Waterside, one of these days.' How could anyone have possibly thought he was mean?

He worked as he walked. He sat on a bench on the towpath or in Bushey Park, scribbling away or learning his lines. One day he was memorizing a sketch about a waiter describing the Celebrity Menu to a restaurant customer. Every item referred to someone in the news at the time.

'What's an Oliver Reed?' asked the client. 'A thick slice of ham marinated overnight in whisky,' replied the waiter. 'What's a Samantha Fox?' 'A game bird, nice plump breasts, very tasty, very sweet.' The second customer asked: 'Enough for two?' And Benny's reply was: 'Oh, ample, madame, ample.'

'I didn't have a voice for this waiter,' he said, 'so I was practising as I walked through the park. I wanted a sort of W.C. Fields with an English accent. It was dusk. I walked out of the park gates and as I did so, I said in a very loud plummy voice, "Nice plump breasts, nice plump breasts!" A man went past on a bicycle and nearly fell off when he heard me. He must have thought all the strange things he'd ever read about me were true.'

14

Benny and Money

Benny had a problem with money. He didn't know what to do with it. He had absolutely no talent for, or interest in, spending it at all. As a boy in Southampton, he had been brought up to be careful with money. But then, so were most working-class children in the thirties during the Depression. His family background was certainly not enough to explain the reputation he earned later on.

You could not fairly describe him as mean, though. People who are mean are generally interested in the accumulation of money, in conserving what they have. Benny had no idea how much he had and certainly did not seek to add to it. It accumulated despite him and once it was there he simply was incapable of spending it.

Once he got rich and his wealth was public knowledge, people started telling stories about legendary acts of meanness from years ago. The problem was, Benny always said, that at the time of these alleged events, he had actually been very poor. There was one tale which was always dragged up whenever there was a new revelation about Benny's wealth. He was supposed to have cadged a lift from a friend to a store where they were selling canned food very cheap. The reason for the dramatic price cut was that all the labels had come off the tins and no one knew whether they were sliced peaches or baked beans. Benny was supposed to have bought a large supply, asked his pal for a lift back home again, and concocted a marvellous meal from his mystery ingredients.

I asked him about it once. There were just two things wrong with the story, he said. He hadn't cadged a lift to the store, he'd gone there under his own steam. And that was in 1948. His Army gratuity was down to the last fourteen pounds. Things were getting desperate. 'It was after that I decided I'd better find some work,' he said.

But even when he did find work as a comic, many similar stories were circulated by his peers. Benny's flat in Maida Vale was supposed to be a cold-water flat because he refused to pay the extra five bob (25p) for hot. It was allegedly furnished with items that had been given to him by furniture stores free in return for declaring a shop open. He must have been doing quite well at this time or he wouldn't have been famous enough to be asked to open shops. Bob Monkhouse said: 'I was told at that time that he had a store of stuff he had been given free. He would open furniture shops in return for goods, and as he hated doing them, he gave poor value for money, because he would just show up, say, "I declare this open", and go.' But there are well-known personalities who still do the same thing to this day. If it was true, he wasn't alone.

They said he also had some items of underwear and perfume he had bought cheap in some job lot which he then gave to the girls he went out with. According to Bob Monkhouse: 'The rumour was that Benny had three kinds of pairs of knickers and shortie nighties, three kinds of long nightgowns, and some bottles of a perfume called Primitif by Max Factor. They said he had acquired a crate of it for doing some kind of service. If a girl had the shortie set, the nightgown and the Primitif, it meant she had been a real hit with Benny Hill! There was one girl who claimed to have several bottles of Primitif.'

There were repeated stories about someone opening a cupboard at his flat and finding piles of uncashed cheques. As is the case with most performers, Benny's fees were paid to his agents. After their commission was deducted, the cheques were sent to the bank to be paid into Benny's two companies, Benny Hill Entertainments Ltd and Benny Hill Productions Ltd, which were administered by his accountants. So it is difficult to know where these cheques came from, if they really existed. Certainly his accountants would send documents for him to sign, and he would leave those lying around, losing money in the process by not signing things in time. He couldn't bring himself to get interested in such things.

Benny's modest lifestyle did not really attract attention for many years. After all, the flat in Queensgate was a highly desirable address and the interior, or part of it at least, elegant enough, thanks to *TV Times.*

When the newspapers compiled lists of the top earners in showbusiness, Benny was never included. The lists were usually put together from different press cuttings about such and such an artist being signed to an exclusive contract worth so much per year. Because of the easy-going nature of his relationship with Thames, without a long-term contract, no announcements were ever made about Benny's deal with the company.

He used to giggle when he read that Jimmy Tarbuck was top of the list. 'I'm OFF the top of it,' he would say. He liked to think he was earning more than some of his colleagues, because it was a measure of how successful his comedy was. He only ever saw his television earnings in this light. Wealth was not an end in itself, just a sign that his work was being recognized.

His agent Richard Stone said: 'He was totally indifferent to money. Oblivious. He liked me to do a good deal for him for the sake of the deal. But what happened to the money after that, he had no idea. We paid the money into his accounts, the accountant invested it for him, and I don't think he had any idea at all of how much money he had got.'

Richard Stone's claim that Benny was earning comparatively little in showbusiness terms until the American deal in the late seventies has to be balanced against the fact that Benny never spent any of his earnings. He did not live up to his income, whatever size it was. He was not interested in cars, property, gadgets, status symbols, or anything else. Ownership caused problems. 'If a thief broke into my house,' he would say, 'all he could take would be my TV and my video. If I had a Rolls-Royce I'd be worrying about it all the time, in case it got scratched or stolen.'

When he travelled abroad, he would often fly first class. But when he got to his destination, he would start using buses, or travel down a French river by cargo boat. It was nothing to do with how much anything cost, it was merely a case of doing whatever he felt like doing. If he felt like flying first class he did. If he felt like going by tube, he did. If he felt like hiring a limo, he did. Whatever fancy took him, he obeyed. He once went to Paris and spent the first night in a £200-a-day hotel, and the next in a tiny £8-per-night 'pension'. Because he felt like it.

Apart from travel costs and meals, he spent no money when he was abroad, because he could not think what to spend it on. He would say plaintively: 'Well, you can only eat one meal at a time, can't you? You can only wear one shirt.' He told me once he had just come back from Paris without spending any money, adding: 'What can you buy in Paris?' I started listing the things you could buy in Paris, finishing up with a Cartier watch. Benny said: 'But I've got a watch.' It was a Swatch, which looked as if it was worth about thirty pounds. I doubt if he could tell the difference between that and a Cartier.

His move to Westrow Gardens in 1986 was done for expediency, and no doubt his claims that he was really going to buy a bigger and better home had some basis in truth. His fondness for walking was perfectly genuine, quite apart from the fact that he believed it would help him lose weight. And his habit of carrying plastic bags was merely one of his more endearing idiosyncrasies. Plastic bags were very handy for carrying videos or scripts, he would say. What else would you carry them in?

The cast of the show gave him an answer when they clubbed together one year and bought him a splendid briefcase. For a joke, they stuffed it full of crumpled plastic carriers. Benny appreciated the thought, but he didn't quite see the point of carrying heavy leather when you could carry lightweight plastic. But the three factors combined – the house, the walking and the plastic bags – were used to turn him into a laughing stock when eventually his real wealth was made public.

In 1988, *Money* magazine published a list of the 200 wealthiest people in Britain based on land values and share-holdings. By now Benny was earning well in excess of a million a year, which in turn was being invested for him. And he was still not spending it. The report claimed Benny had a personal fortune of £10 million, quoting the profits of his company, Benny Hill Entertainments Ltd, at £933,073 after tax for the year 1986–7.

The tabloid stories which followed hurt him deeply. He was described as Britain's meanest man, living variously in a 'crumbling council house', or a 'shabby semi', walking everywhere or travelling by bus to save taxi fares, and shambling about carrying plastic bags like a tramp. When one paper dug up the fact that he had been visiting Sue Upton's home in Hornchurch, they even used that against him and claimed he went to Essex for his holidays because he was so mean.

Benny's first reaction to the *Money* magazine story was amazement that anyone could invade his privacy in this way. His press cuttings service had already sent him a story from a Sri Lankan publication claiming he was worth £10 million, and at first he thought *Money* magazine had simply copied it. He dismissed the list as worthless if they 'did their research in Sri Lanka'. He did not know that they could check on the assets of his companies at Companies House. When he had this explained to him, he started saying that they were still wrong. 'They're a hundred per cent wrong,' he told me. He wouldn't elaborate. He might have meant that they had only quoted one of his companies, instead of two. He might have thought they meant £10 million in cash in the bank, which he didn't have since it was all invested, and that they were therefore wrong on this count. Whatever he thought of the report, he could not get away from it. All the old stories about the cans of food and the simple TV-watching lifestyle were dragged up, and pictures were snatched of him walking to the studios with his carrier bags. The instant tabloid label of the meanest millionaire stuck with him for ever.

His friends leaped to his defence with stories about acts of generosity over the years but these did not make very good copy, especially since no one could come up with an example of out and out extravagance.

'I used to be called a sexist, now I'm a tightwad,' he moaned to me. 'I'm so used to having rubbish written about me, exclusive interviews with people I've never spoken to, so how can I take any of this seriously?'

His mood soon lightened. We were sitting in a restaurant in Teddington High Street one day having lunch. I was reading the menu when he suddenly said: 'Phew, it's hot in here, isn't it?' I carried on reading. Then he said: 'My word, it's hot, don't you find it hot?' He obviously wanted me to look up at him. He was fanning himself vigorously with a 'fan' of £50 notes to prove that he was no miser. Normally he never carried more than £150 or £200 in cash on him. He'd picked up £600 at the bank specially for the joke.

It was my turn to get hot under the collar a few minutes later. On holiday in Italy, I had seen in a lingerie shop a strange garment consisting of stockings and suspenders all in one. I suppose it was really tights with the tops cut out into the shape of lacy suspenders. I thought it would make Benny laugh, so I bought it. I was wearing it that day we had lunch in Teddington. I started carefully pulling my skirt up to show him, but I knew I had accidentally gone too far when I saw the beaming smile flash across his face. 'You have just made an old man very happy,' he said.

He carried on doing the joke with the money for other people. During rehearsals he would suddenly pull a great wad of £50 notes out of one of his plastic carriers and fan himself. 'He did it several times and I thought he was getting a bit eccentric,' confessed Bob Todd.

I suggested one day he could get himself a better press by lavishing some extravagant gifts on the girls he took out. 'I do already,' he said indignantly. 'I always buy them a newspaper.' At least he was seeing the funny side of the whole thing.

Once the world knew the extent of his wealth, people started asking about his will. He had no obvious heir. At work, they made jokes about it all the time. Anyone who pulled a chair out for him or offered some small act of kindness was told: 'Yes, little heart, you'll be in the will.' In fact, he had not made a will since 1961, and that left everything to his parents, who both predeceased him. In retrospect, it seems odd that someone with so much money had not made provision for its disposition. It would have been a chance at last for him to prove that he was not mean by making some generous bequests. But it was probably just a question of not having got round to it.

He told several people quite seriously that he intended to make one. One day he was on the ferry at Hamble with his cousin Chris. 'There was no one else on it, and we were having one of those serious conversations that you have when there's no danger of anyone hearing,' said Chris. 'It wasn't the sort of thing we would normally talk about, but he did say that he thought he'd better alter the will he had made because it was out of date. I didn't even know that he'd made one in the first place.' He continued telling people he was just about to make a new will right up until his death.

15

Hill's Little Angels

Of all the members of 'the family', Benny was probably closest to Sue Upton, who had been with the show since she was twenty. She made Benny laugh. She had her own special brand of malapropisms and would come out with wonderfully mixed-up expressions, which Benny called Uptons. He always claimed that he was going to publish a book of them when he had compiled enough. But he also took to her simplicity and straightforwardness. There was a total lack of pretention about Sue which put the strange world of television and showbusiness in its proper perspective.

Their closeness was apparent to everyone. They walked arm in arm or hand in hand. He chatted to her on the phone for hours and socialized with her outside the show far more than he did with anyone else. He talked about her constantly.

They became such confidants that some of 'the family' thought Sue could have become Mrs Hill under different circumstances. But Benny had long since given up the idea of marriage by the time he met her. He just doted on her because she represented everything he liked in a girl. She took her work on the show seriously but she remained unspoiled, unsophisticated, trustworthy. 'I think Benny liked her because she never changed,' said Jenny Lee-

Wright. 'She was always the same innocent, down-to-earth Sue, completely herself, and he really appreciated that.'

Sue was already engaged when she joined the show, and married quite soon afterwards. At first, she didn't want Benny to know about her wedding plans. He so often disapproved of girls who put love and marriage before a career. But Benny made an exception for his sweet Sue and became very friendly with her husband, painter and decorator Roger Whatling. Before long they had two children, Richard and Louise.

Soon after Richard was born Benny visited Sue in hospital, and swamped her with flowers. But he was too nervous to hold the baby.

Sue worked hard to get her figure back after Richard's birth and was soon back as Benny's chief Angel. Benny insisted on her being in the show even when she was visibly pregnant with her second child, Louise.

Ever afterwards he would refer to her as Mum or 'the old mother hen', when she fussed over him and reminded him to go for a medical check-up or watch his diet. She knew instinctively when her closeness was welcome and when he wanted her to back off a little.

Benny grew to rely on Sue for a lot. Professionally, he asked her to look for new girls for the show. Privately, he occasionally asked her to arrange dates for him. On a domestic level, it was Sue and Roger who helped him move when he left London, Sue who looked at new houses, Sue who advised him on this and that; Roger was was trusted to mastermind the redecoration of Benny's sanctuary in Southampton.

Sue and Roger lived in Hornchurch, Essex, and it was there Benny would go and stay whenever he had a few free days. With them he found the nearest thing to a real home life he'd tasted since he was fifteen. The Whatlings became his substitute family and he was a regular visitor. 'I must be one of the few women who can say they've taken Benny Hill coffee and biscuits in bed,' Sue would say, a claim that was probably nearer the truth than the picture Benny still tried to paint of a constant stream of women filing through his bedroom.

If Sue didn't go in to wake him up in the morning, the children would. He'd take them to playschool, throw balls in the garden for them. He was the indulgent present-buying uncle who'd missed out on fatherhood himself and was now making up for it. When Richard started infant school, Benny would go to meet him, standing waiting at the school gates with all the young mums. But as ever, work was never far from his mind. If Richard or Louise did something funny or made a droll remark, out would come Benny's notebook and he would write it down.

However, it wasn't Sue's youngsters who first gave him the idea of including children in the show. That had happened when another of his former show girls, Jenny Westbrook, took her baby daughter, Jade, round to the flat in Queensgate for tea. Benny was terribly excited about it and keen to do everything exactly right, but it was his first real contact with a toddler and he had no idea what they ate or drank. In the end, he told me, he bought a bottle of nearly all the soft drinks the shop had on sale, and every kind of biscuit and cake.

Jade Westbrook was an exceptionally cute child, with huge eyes, dark curls and chubby limbs. Benny was entranced by her. Soon after that first tea-party, they all went to the circus, and little Jade sat on his knee.

'She is so sweet,' he enthused to me afterwards. She was also very photogenic and receptive to direction. He decided to try her out in the show. She made her début on her second birthday and it worked so well he decided to expand her role in future shows. There was one lovely shot where they walked off together, backs to the camera, her fat little legs struggling to keep pace with his.

Now he got the idea of using more children, but he did not want professional stage-school youngsters. To Jade he added Sue's two, Richard and Louise, choreographer Libby Roberts' son, Adam Johnstone, and Dennis Kirkland's daughter Joanna. Dennis would tell her: 'You're not the director's daughter now, kid, you're one of the team, so get out there and act your socks off.'

Using the children, dubbed Hill's Little Angels, was one of Benny's ways of cleaning up the show. He cut down on the raunchy dance numbers, and lengthened the sketches featuring the kids. He seriously thought that this would deflect the mounting criticism about the sexiness of the show's content.

It was painstaking work getting the children to do everything right. Usually their sketches were silent, but sometimes he gave them lines. Sue Upton remembered Louise having a line in a tea-party sketch when she had to say to Benny the Butler: 'I'd like some of those nice little triangular cucumber sandwiches with the crusts cut off.' There was much lengthy coaching. Then one night Sue went into Louise's bedroom and heard her saying in her sleep: 'I'd like some of those nice little triangular cucumber sandwiches ...'

Not all the adult members of the cast and crew were as pleased as Benny was with the use of the kids. They thought it took far too long to get their scenes right, and that their own input was being reduced as a result. But some of it was very Chaplinesque. Richard Whatling, his baseball cap stuck on the side of his head, his hair sticking up like a Dennis the Menace cartoon, played Jackie Coogan to Benny's Charlie.

Most important of all for Benny was that the children added a new element to his private life. As well as filming with him in the summer, they had a regular date with Benny every Christmas holiday, when he took them all to a pantomime. The outing always included a meal for the Little Angels and their parents. 'I choose one of those restaurants where kids are allowed to stuff their faces,' he said. On one occasion, Benny forgot to take off his paper hat after the meal, and solemnly walked to the theatre and sat throughout the performance still wearing it.

'I look forward to seeing the littlies so much,' he said. 'I absolutely love them. I suppose sometimes it does make me regret having none of my own.' Then, pragmatic as ever, he added: 'Of course, I just see them at their best. Maybe if they were crying at three o'clock in the morning, it might not seem such fun.'

16

His Own Worst Enemy

In 1979 Benny had added an extra element to the show. Much taken with the suspender-clad dance group Hot Gossip, whose routines spiced up the comedy in 'The Kenny Everett Show', Benny was also impressed by Everett's claim that the dancers had boosted his audience figures. He invented his own group, composed of very pretty young dancers, first as a parody of Hot Gossip and then as a feature in their own right. He called them Hill's Angels, partly as a pun on the old movie title, *Hell's Angels*, and partly as a twist on 'Charlie's Angels', an American TV programme popular at the time, about a team of pretty girl investigators dominated by an unseen man. The image he had sought since he had seen that first comic in Southampton over forty-five years earlier was now complete. Few commentators ever referred to Benny again without also mentioning the Angels.

But in the 1980s the show began to run into problems with criticism about the sexiness of the content. At first there were a few amicable exchanges with the Independent Broadcasting Authority about the dance sequences. At one point, there was a complaint about the way shots were angled between the girls' legs, so they appeared to be backing on to the camera. This was thought not to be a good idea.

Dennis Kirkland was told not to repeat a costume which had a see-through top. Nipples were not allowed on 'The Benny Hill Show'. The frames including that particular girl had to be excised from the dance sequence when the show was repeated. But that left the film too short for the music track. A shot of another girl sliding down a pole was 'stretched' slightly to fill the gap, so that the girl seemed to jerk down the pole rather than slide. It looked sexier, in the end, than a see-through top.

Kirkland had initially tried to make the girls look as raunchy as possible because he thought this would help sell the show to the American audience.

Jon Jon Keefe had a friend who lived in the Florida Everglades who had asked for a photo of Keefe with Benny to put up in his living-room: 'One day a man came to hang his new curtains. He saw the photo and realized my friend actually knew someone who knew Benny Hill. He said, "That guy has given me so much joy, and I've never seen so much bare flesh in my living-room in my life. So you can have the drapes for nothing." That's how the Americans were about it. But Benny didn't always approve of what was happening to the girls' costumes. He'd say, "Oh no, Den, dear heart, we can't have them looking like that." Den took the responsibility for making the costumes sexier but Benny got the brickbats afterwards.'

If Benny found out that any of the girls were unhappy with what they were supposed to wear, he put a stop to it right away. Bob Todd remembered; 'One day the dancers had been given costumes by the designers where the bit of material in the crotch was only about two inches wide. One of them came to me and said, "We can't wear these, we're too embarrassed." ' So tactful Toddy went to Benny and casually mentioned what a pity it was that the

At the end of a long trip up the mountain above Montreux, a frozen Benny poses with Dennis Kirkland, May 1985.

With the author, in Thorpe Park, Surrey, in 1987.

girls were upset about the costumes. 'I said they were terrified to wear them in case they showed too much. He sent for the wardrobe mistress immediately and ordered them to be changed without even seeing them. He was like a Dutch uncle to those girls.'

There was still a feeling that there was something 'not quite nice' about 'The Benny Hill Show'. Philip Jones remembers attending a forum at the Edinburgh TV Festival and hearing Benny's shows being attacked for being anti-feminist. 'You sit there trying to answer it, and you realize you might as well save your breath because these ladies have made up their minds. It suddenly became fashionable to start knocking him.'

The ratings for the show were no longer as high as they had once been. The new fashion in television was for soap operas and these tended to dominate the top half of the TV ratings chart. And a decision had been made to add a series of half-hour repeats to the brand-new specials Benny did each year. These inevitably debased the currency slightly. Benny was no longer a rare treat. Nevertheless, the audience figures held up well under the circumstances. His last three shows screened in 1989 got audiences of eleven million, ten million and nine and a half million, still respectable audiences for comedy at a time when audiences were crying out for soap, soap and more soap.

In spite of all this there was now a growing feeling among the younger generation of Thames executives that Benny had simply been around too long. The new fashion was for the young and trendy. Philip Jones could sense a wind of change blowing through Thames' thinking about entertainment. Not just the man due to take over from him, John Howard Davies, but others, such as Director of Programmes David Elstein, were looking enviously towards the BBC and some of its more 'alternative' comedy.

One example always cited was the 'Blackadder' historical comedy series starring and partly conceived by one of the young Oxbridge comics, Rowan Atkinson. 'Blackadder' had not always been a success. Its first series, in which Blackadder was a fifteenth century prince, was made largely on film with all the attendant costs. It was so pricey that it had caused resentments in other departments of the BBC not gifted with the same lavish budgets. The resentment grew when the show was not even a big ratings success.

It faded from view for a while. But the BBC has a way of persevering with things that the more commercially orientated (at least in those days) ITV had always admired. They brought 'Blackadder' back, revamped it and made it a studio-based show to reduce costs. Each series was set in a different historical period, culminating in a series set in the First World War trenches of Northern France. Now the BBC found themselves with a massive, critically acclaimed hit on their hands.

This was the sort of show Thames, and most of the other ITV companies, wanted to do. It was very funny, very clever, often outrageously rude, yet with a literate and intellectual base which made it an acceptable dinner party subject among the chattering classes.

Thames have yet to achieve anything quite in this league, but shortly after Benny left, they did bring in Rowan Atkinson himself to make occasional near-silent half-hour films featuring his hilariously nerdish nose-picking character, Mr Bean. These went on to win the sort of audiences, foreign sales and prizes – including the 1990 Golden Rose of Montreux – which Benny had once enjoyed.

In March 1988, Philip Jones retired as Controller of Light Entertainment. He would still be retained as a consultant, and another of his plans was to team up with Don Taffner and make some situation comedies independently. His successor, John Howard Davies, was a former child actor and the star of *Oliver Twist*. As a comedy producer he had made his name with some of the BBC's most successful programmes like 'The Good Life' and 'Fawlty Towers'. At the BBC he had risen to head of the Light Entertainment department before leaving to go to Thames once more as a situation comedy producer and director. He always claimed that this was his real love. But everyone felt he was all the time being kept in the wings ready to take over from Philip Jones.

For years Benny had tended to end any sketch about an actor or a TV director, or anything featuring a TV studio, by walking off into the wings shouting anxiously 'Philip!', a small homage to the man who had been so important in his career. When Philip wrote to tell Benny he was leaving, Benny replied on his usual lined paper. 'How the time has flown,' he wrote.'It always does when you're having fun. I am pleased you will still be around, albeit in a different capacity. It'll still be "Philip!!!!", "John Howard!!!" just doesn't sound the same.' Then he added: 'If you feel I could help/take part/write or whatever, with your future projects, with or without Thames, well, you know where I can be found.' It was more prophetic than he realized at the time.

Under the new regime, things started quite well. The Benny Hill unit was filming at the sports club next door to Thames' studios when John Howard Davies walked over to introduce himself to Benny. Benny was as distracted as ever when he was working. 'I don't think he really grasped who it was he was shaking hands with,' said Jon Jon Keefe. John Howard Davies initially reiterated the old Thames line about Benny being the jewel in the crown, certainly of his own department.

Benny's fee for each show had never been very high compared with other stars like Morecambe and Wise, and London Weekend's Jimmy Tarbuck. He preferred departmental money to go into the budget for the show. After all, he made more than he could ever need from the overseas sales. But the first thing John did was to give him a rise. 'He told me Benny was underpaid and gave him a rise, virtually without me asking for it,' said Richard Stone.

The climate was now turning faster than ever against shows like Benny's. The readers of a woman's magazine voted it their least favourite show. Many women were heard to dismiss it as smutty. But the smut was mostly in the eye of the beholder. It was, as ever, all innuendo, never explicit.

One of the young comedians who were pushing their way to the front in a great bursting wave of new talent had started another ball rolling when he mentioned Benny in ·an interview. Ben Elton, the son of a university academic and a teacher, and himself a graduate of Manchester University, questioned whether it was a good idea, at a time when it was not safe for women to walk in parks because of the increasing incidence of rape, for Benny to be seen chasing half-naked girls through parks. He repeated the idea in his act.

Benny's first reaction was outrage that someone had broken the showbusiness code: that one comic should not criticize another. Dennis Kirkland at first tried to stop Benny from discussing it with me. 'Are you sure you want to say this?' he queried, thinking Benny was about to commit the same crime by attacking Ben. 'No, it's important that I say it,' Benny told him.

He refused to mention Ben Elton, or anyone else who had jumped on this particular bandwagon, by name. So he went through the whole conversation with no one being identified but both of us knowing very well to whom he was referring. Even so it was said more in sorrow than in anger. 'I have done my own show now for about thirty-five years but I have never run down a fellow performer, except for the joke I used to do with Bob Monkhouse where we slagged one another off like Hope and Crosby. But that was agreed between the two of us,' he said. 'I would never make a serious criticism of another comic. Never. Never. Never.' He was really vehement. 'But several of the newer performers, because they have not got much of a background in showbusiness, don't know the rules. They have been slagging me off. Personally, I think they're like little boys in school. "Johnny, did you break that window?" "Yes, miss, but HE broke one as well." It's to divert criticism from themselves by deflecting in on to me. You just don't do that!! They criticize me for chasing girls through a park, when in real life it's not safe for girls to walk through parks alone. If they watched the show properly, they would see it's always girls chasing me. Their material is outrageous. They do jokes about men having periods!' (He was deeply shocked by this.) 'Then they turn round to *TV Times* and criticize me!'

Benny claimed to have watched one 'alternative' comedy show where there was a naked man bouncing up and down on another man's lap. 'And they have the nerve to criticize me,' he spluttered. He had even been shocked by an act which consisted of three naked men covering their private parts with balloons. 'It's not a pretty sight,' he said, 'certainly not as pretty as our girls in bikinis.'

He was also taken aback by the violence of some of the new acts, such as Rik Mayall and Ade Edmondson's Dangerous Brothers. 'There was another moment when one man embedded an axe with great force in another man's groin,' he said. 'I thought for a minute there I was seeing my first snuff movie [a film in which someone is actually killed]. I was so amazed, I ran the tape back to make sure what I'd seen.'

Even though he couldn't always approve of the content of their acts, he still liked the 'alternatives'. He loved the anarchic Liverpudlian Alexei Sayle, and was very thrilled when he was invited to present an Emmy in New York to Alexei some time later. He also particularly liked two double acts, Stephen Fry and Hugh Laurie, and Gareth Hale and Norman Pace. He still knew talent when he saw it.

He wanted the young generation to leave him alone, even if they could not appreciate him the way he admired them. 'There's enough TV critics and people out there with their own points of view, without performers doing it to each other,' he said. There was also a well-known producer and director who rarely missed an opportunity to hurl a few public brickbats at the content of 'The Benny Hill Show'.

Benny's annoyance at what he regarded as bad manners blinded him to real criticism. He never stopped to ask himself if any of them had a point. He dismissed the whole thing far too easily. He seized on the one mistake they made. In the speeded-up run-off at the end of the show, it was not Benny chasing girls, it was always the rest of the cast chasing Benny.

He thought that because they were wrong over this one

fact, it meant they never watched the show and therefore did not know what they were talking about. This negated everything they said. Unfortunately, by narrowing the argument to this one disputed strand, he failed to appreciate that there were bits in the show which were likely to make many women wince. There was a repeated theme of old men lusting after very young girls. It may be 'ageist' to say so, but it was not always a pretty sight either, despite Benny's precious bikinis. Benny could not see that a sketch where a man made a play for a beautiful young girl and ended up instead with a plain older woman was offensive to some women. He thought it was a joke at the expense of the man.

I recall one very pertinent sketch where he portrayed men as circus animals in thrall to female lion-tamers and ring-masters. But on the whole, the female sex was portrayed in his shows the way he himself saw women – as wives, girlfriends, objects of lust or mere decoration. He simply did not know what sexism meant.

In the way he responded to the continual charges of sexism, he became his own worst enemy. A well-argued feminist attack on the show would leave him floundering. He would answer it with silly jokes about feminism and masculinism.

Bob Monkhouse told me: 'I can never really forgive the pseudo-intellectuals who castigated him in the later years of so-called political correctness, because they really hurt him. But his defences were puerile, and I was embarrassed by them. I wanted to say, "Shut up, and just don't join in the same game. Just know that we love you and everyone who has ever worked with you cares for you. And those of us who are practitioners of comedy know you as a towering exemplar of British comedy." Which he was.'

In the spring of 1989, Colin Shaw, ex-director of pro-grammes at the IBA and now director of the new Broad-casting Standards Council, gave an interview in which he mentioned 'The Benny Hill Show': 'It is no longer as funny as it once was to have dirty old men chasing half-naked girls across the screen,' he stated. Colin Shaw says now that the comment in that first interview was purely a personal opinion. There had been no dialogue with Thames about the show, and there was no question that the Council planned to 'go after' Benny.

The BSC was to be the government's new watchdog, dealing with complaints about bad taste, violence and bad language on TV and radio. It was a sort of official Mary Whitehouse, and the television industry was very nervous of how powerful it was going to be. In fact, when the Council published its Code of Practice in November 1989, it said: 'Although the half-undressed young woman has been a staple element in farce and light entertainment shows, the convention is becoming increasingly offensive to a growing number of people and should be used only sparingly.' There was no direct reference to Benny's shows, and never intended to be, says Shaw. Too much, he thinks, was perhaps read into one line in one interview. If anything, Thames' subsequent action over Benny was a response not to him, but to a general feeling in the air at the time.

Thames had probably already made up their minds about their future course of action when Shaw's interview was published. But Benny took it very personally indeed. He thought the BSC was being set up to get him, and was furious that nobody seemed to notice that he too was aware of the mood of the times, and was trying to respond to it.

He claimed that by then he had one of the cleanest

shows on TV. He had sensed the new climate at least four years earlier, and had started phasing out the sexy dance routines, replacing them with the sequences with the Little Angels. Even suspenders were out. He told me: 'The women's libbers are forever having a go at me, so I think perhaps the time has come when one shouldn't be so raunchy. I changed the show because it was the time to change. You'll be lucky if you spot a single suspender in the latest show. Well, maybe one ... I saw the way opinion was going, and when people want hula hoops you sell them hula hoops. It's a question of what is in vogue at the moment and keeping in touch with public taste.'

Then he fell back on his same old defence. 'Those who criticize me definitely haven't seen the show because I never ever chase girls. Anyway, over thirteen million people still watch my shows in this country so I must be doing something right.' He thought it was all as insignificant as a row in the very early days of TV which he was fond of citing as an example of how stupidly people get wound up about the most innocuous things if they're on a TV screen.

In the early fifties, one of the panellists on 'What's My Line', Ron Randell, had blown a kiss to the camera at the end of a show. It caused outrage. 'Colonels in Chipping Sodbury wrote to the newspapers saying that their thirteen-year-old daughters had come in crying because a man on the telly had tried to kiss them,' Benny recounted gleefully. 'If Colin Shaw had been around at the time he would probably have had a heart attack.'

Afterwards, Randell was always referred to in the newspapers as Ron 'Kiss' Randell. Some years later, Benny had been dining in the Caprice with his air hostess girlfriend when they had met Randell and discussed the 'scandal'. 'Well, Benny,' said Ron, 'all I can say is that I'm still dining at the Caprice.' Benny was convinced that he would weather these silly little storms too. Metaphorically speaking, he would still be 'dining at the Caprice' in television terms for some time to come. 'It doesn't mean anything to me. I'll be doing three new specials as usual next year,' he said. 'And probably the year after that. After all, Thames are not going to turn round and say they don't want me any more, just because of a bit of criticism in the papers, are they? My darling, it's all water off a duck's back.'

Six weeks after our conversation he discovered just how wrong he was.

17

Sacked

In April 1989, Thames invited Benny to attend the MIP-TV Festival, a programme sales market for TV companies from all over the world, held in Cannes. Thames were pushing the boat out at MIP because it was their coming of age.

Being paraded in this way was not something he enjoyed, but because he thought it would help Thames, and because it was in the South of France, which he loved, he agreed to go. Thames Television International, the company's sales arm, issued a press release which was positively gushing in its effusiveness: 'Benny Hill, the world's most successful comedian and Thames' longest-serving artist, will be attending this year's MIP-TV for the first time from Friday 21 April to Monday 24 April as part of Thames Television's twenty-first anniversary,' it began. It went on to describe Benny as 'a world legend in his own lifetime', and 'a genius'. It said that his show had topped TV ratings all over the world and still had audiences 'begging for more'. Only Thames wasn't begging for more, it transpired.

Benny was given a massive luxury suite at Loew's Hotel, at La Napoule near Cannes. It was full of flowers. When he saw it, modest as ever, he said: 'Oh you didn't need to go to all this trouble for me, any room would have done.'

He was treated like the star of the hour. In fact, he was the only one of Thames' stars attending this prestigious occasion, and when he walked into the reception at Le Château in La Napoule, the buyers from the foreign TV stations absolutely flocked around him.

Don Taffner was there and introduced him to Walter Cronkite. John Howard Davies was there, and mentioned to Benny that they had to have a talk when they got home. Benny assumed it was either the production go-ahead he had been waiting for, or some fresh promotional exercise they wanted him to do. But many of those who worked for Thames Television International had got wind of a rumour that there was something odd happening behind the scenes.

'Do you know what's going on with Benny Hill?' they kept asking people from the Thames production side. It was not just idle curiosity. 'The Benny Hill Show' was their big sales weapon. They needed it. Surely it wasn't in danger?

Benny himself was blissfully unaware of all this. He returned to London still thinking he was 'the jewel in Thames' crown', and anxiously waiting to be given the go-ahead for filming to begin on the new shows. He could not understand what the delay was.

The third and final show of those already in the can for 1989 was screened on 1 May, and possibly this was what Thames were waiting for. After all, they could hardly sack a man then screen one of his shows in prime time a few weeks' later. The Annual General Meeting was also approaching. Possibly they wanted to get that out of the way too.

Meanwhile, Richard Stone read a newspaper report of

something John Howard Davies was supposed to have said about making sweeping changes in his department. He felt uneasy about it, and tried to call John to clarify any future plans regarding Benny. 'I'd known John since he was a schoolboy, he was at school with my sons,' Richard said. 'I put in a call to him and asked for him to phone back. He didn't call.'

On Thursday 25 May Thames announced pre-tax profits of £31 million in the year to the end of March. From sales of 'The Benny Hill Show' to America alone, they had made £1 million, though this was much less than the previous year. But new markets were opening up for the show. It had recently been seen in Russia for the first time.

The following week Benny and Dennis were summoned to see John Howard Davis in his office at Teddington. They thought it was a production meeting to finalize budgets and filming schedules for the new shows and arrived in high spirits. As they went into the outer office of John Howard Davies' empire, where the secretaries sat, they did their usual Laurel and Hardy fat man, thin man joke, pretending to get wedged in the door. After you, Stan. No, after you, Ollie.

Benny was invited in first. Five minutes later, he came out, straight-faced. 'He wants to see you now,' he told Dennis. 'He's got a bit of a surprise for you.' Benny waited till Dennis emerged after an equally brief interview. They looked at one another. 'I need a drink,' said Benny. 'Me too,' said Kirkland. For once they left the room without doing any jokes for the benefit of the secretaries. Avoiding the Anglers pub next door to the studio, where they might bump into too many Thames staff, they made their way hastily to the King's Head in Teddington High Street. 'And there,' Benny told me later, 'we got a bit drunk.'

Meanwhile, Richard Stone was working on his allot-
ment above his home in Seaview, Isle of Wight, when his
wife came running up from the house to say that John
Howard Davies had returned his call at last. 'He said he
had just talked to Benny. He said, "I'm sorry Richard, but
I've had to tell him I don't want the show any more."
Then he said something like, "We've come to the end of
the line, let's quit while we're winning." '

He didn't give any justification for the decision. Three
years later, Stone is still shocked by the way the matter
was handled. 'He could have called both of us in or taken
me out to lunch and said it was getting too expensive and
discussed what we were going to do. But he didn't even
return my calls. Instead he just called Benny in like a
schoolboy. If there could ever be a more appalling way of
ending an association with your major star, I've never
heard of one.'

A few minutes later Benny phoned Richard himself. 'I
was really touched that he called me so quickly. It showed
that there really was a bond between us despite everything. But he was shattered, absolutely shattered. He
couldn't believe what had been done or the way it had
been done.'

Philip Jones phoned Benny that same day. 'Comics are
insecure creatures at the best of times,' he said, 'but it had
hurt Benny particularly badly because it had come as
such a surprise. He kept on about how they had taken
him to Cannes and made such a fuss of him.'

John Howard Davies might have been the executioner
but he was not judge and jury The only thing he has ever
said to me about it since is that the decision was not his
alone. Undoubtedly it was made in conjunction with his
programme controller, though it is thought that Richard
Dunn, then managing director and now chief executive,

was not party to it. But no one ever put their hands up to the deed, and the company never issued any formal statement.

Instead, with newspapers already sniffing around, Roy Addison and Melanie Louis in Thames' press office, together with Richard Stone, concocted a story that Benny had decided to take some time off work. Addison's office was known for its maxim: 'Never lie to the press, they always find out the truth in the end.' The white lie on this occasion was really a vain attempt to protect Benny from the ignominy of having everyone in the world know that he had been sacked. But the exclusive in the *Daily Mirror* on 31 May made it sound as if Benny had walked out. 'He has told his bosses at Thames TV that he doesn't want to make any more programmes for at least a year,' it said. 'He wants a complete rest from showbusiness.' The follow-up in the *Sun* said that Benny had decided to retire because he thought he was too old to keep up the pace. The *Daily Star* went further. It claimed that Benny had completely 'stunned Thames TV bosses when he refused to renew his yearly contract'.

I picked up the papers that morning and didn't believe a word of it. I knew that he had been desperate to get back to work. I phoned him at the flat. He said: 'I'm not supposed to talk to you, my darling. I've had to agree the press office will handle everything.' His voice was wobbly.

By the weekend the real story of the sacking had emerged, and the Sunday papers gave a more truthful version.

Benny received many letters from staff at Thames saying how badly they thought he had been treated, but nothing from anyone at executive level. 'I was in and out in two minutes,' he told me. 'You would have thought I'd

get a lunch or some little pat on the back after twenty-
one years.'

Some members of 'the family' were too embarrassed to
ring Benny. They thought commiseration would only add
to his humiliation. But others were there to cushion him.
He had already made arrangements to go and see Louise
English at the Mill Theatre at Sonning, where she was
appearing in a musical, and then to stay with Sue Upton
for a few days.

When Louise read the papers, she didn't think he'd
turn up, but he did, along with Sue. They all went to
lunch at the Compleat Angler, one of Benny's favourites
in nearby Marlow, before the show. 'He was totally bewild-
ered by what had happened. It was a terrible thing to do
to him,' said Louise. 'I felt so bad for him. If only there
was something I could have done to relieve the pain for
that man. I was angry on his behalf. I said, "What are you
going to do about it?" He said, "Nothing little heart, they
have their reasons. What can I do?" He was so hurt.'
Immediately afterwards Benny went to stay for a few
days at Sue Upton's home at Hornchurch.

He wrote to Sylvia Thorley to tell her his plans and said
he was looking forward to taking 'the littlies' to the beach
and the circus. He added: 'By the way, don't take too
much notice of what the press are writing about me. I am
not retiring. I have not been banned. I haven't bought a
villa in Outer Mongolia.'

Other friends were rallying round too. Within days of
the sacking, Richard Stone, Philip Jones and Don Taffner
had got together to discuss the idea of making the show
as an independent production company. They had lunch
with Benny at the White Elephant in Mayfair.

'Benny looked as if he had been mugged,' said Don.
'He couldn't understand what was going on. He was

really, really sad and confused. If people hadn't rallied round, I don't know what would have happened to him. I mean, engagements break, marriages end in divorce, partnerships end, but there are ways of doing it that are much nicer than the way Thames did it. There were several of us around that were really pissed off with them about it, more so than Benny was. He was just sad and hurt. That was the period where Dennis was really supportive to him. In fact, he became a necessity to him.'

Kirkland also found himself rather freer than he'd anticipated to look after Benny's welfare. A few weeks after Benny's sacking, he was called in again and told that Thames had no work for him in the foreseeable future, although his contract had over twelve months to run. He was given a year's pay and accompanied Benny into the wilderness. It meant he was available to produce and direct the independent project if it got off the ground.

The first thing Philip Jones did was write to his old friend and Thames colleague Brian Tesler, now boss of London Weekend Television, proposing a Benny Hill show to be made as an independent production for LWT, and channelled by them on to the network. Independent productions, once a rarity, were now increasingly common since the government had obliged the TV companies to take twenty-five per cent of their programming from the independent sector. London Weekend were very interested in the proposition. Both programme controller Greg Dyke and light entertainment chief Marcus Plantin thought Benny's brand of variety would play very well on a Saturday night.

The company had just opened up its facilities to independent productions for the first time, and now they checked there would be studio space available to make 'The New Benny Hill Show'. In spite of the fact that some people in the company were a bit sniffy about it, Plantin and Dyke fought it through. The plan was to make six half-hours with the option of more.

All they had to do was get the plan approved by the ITV network. At that time, ITV operated a complex system whereby the amount of time each regional station was allowed on the full ITV network was in direct proportion to the power and financial muscle of the company.

The schedules were dominated by the Big Five – Thames, Granada, Central, London Weekend and York-shire – which all had 'guaranteed time' when their pro-grammes got a prime slot automatically. The smaller companies had to fight an often losing battle to get their shows into peak-time viewing, regardless of the actual quality of the product.

Of course, many of the Big Five programmes fully deserved their place in the schedules. But the smaller companies believed that the system was utterly unfair to them. Even if they had a programme of quality which they felt merited a place in the national schedule, they often could not get it on because their much smaller advertising income worked against them.

So after a lot of lobbying by companies like TVS and Scottish, a new system was being tried out. In addition to the 'guaranteed time' which was still the province of the Big Five, the network had set aside certain hours which were in theory open to any company. This was known as the Flexipool, and a subcommittee was set up in each programme area – drama, light entertainment, factual, etc – to arbitrate over submissions.

In the summer of 1989, Marcus Plantin, then head of London Weekend's powerful light entertainment div-ision, took a project to the Flexipool. He would finance a package of six Benny Hill shows to be produced inde-

pendently by Taffner UK Ltd, provided the network
would accept it. The subcommittee at that time comprised
representatives from London Weekend (Plantin himself),
Yorkshire TV, Scottish TV, Granada, TVS, Central and
Thames, which was represented by John Howard Davies.

If the Flexipool had given the go ahead, the shows
would certainly have been destined for Saturday nights.
Thames, in those days, held the franchise for the London
area on weekdays only, up until about 6 p.m. on Friday. So
what happened at weekends did not theoretically concern
them since they were not on the air.

John Howard Davies did not vote on Plantin's plan,
but he joined in the discussion. The committee was not
enthusiastic. They'd all heard the claims that Benny was
sexist and old-fashioned. They'd all read what the Broadcasting Standards Council apparently thought. They'd all
been to the Edinburgh TV festival and heard what the
politically correct attitude was. They didn't want to sound
like yesterday's men. Plantin argued his case but the vote
went against him. Plantin reluctantly withdrew. Benny
was back in the market.

The Taffner project was then offered to the BBC. But
their response was rather dog in the manger. Benny had
been one of their major stars before Thames had snaffled
him twenty years earlier. Now that Thames had decided
to sack him, why should they pick up the pieces? They
regarded him as someone else's cast-off.

Richard Stone says: 'Thames' action in dropping Benny
effectively killed his career as far as British TV was concerned for over two years. It did enormous damage.' But
Don Taffner had made an absolute commitment to make
a show for the American market, no matter what the
British TV companies might do. Plans for that went
ahead.

Benny was sustained, too, by several newspaper polls which asked their readers whether Thames had been right to sack Benny. The indications were that the viewers still wanted to see Benny. It was just the TV companies who weren't willing to let them do it. Benny clung to the belief that his public, somewhere, still loved him and it just about kept him going.

18

The Wandering Years

Don Taffner and Philip Jones were still determined that the new Benny Hill show would get made somehow. Don decided to finance the first one himself and aim it directly at the American market. The new plan was to make a series called 'The World of Benny Hill', or 'Benny Hill's World Tour', getting finance from different sources around the world. Each show would have a slight flavour of the country involved, with Benny filming a few scenes locally. They hoped to make one in Paris and one in Berlin, maybe one in Australia, and one other. But despite the international colour, the bulk of the new shows would be the mixture as before.

Marcus Plantin, shortly to become LWT's director of programmes, was still interested in getting Benny back on to British TV. He thought that since the new shows would be financed from abroad, it might be possible to buy them as part of London Weekend's foreign acquisitions quota, a fixed percentage of programming which British networks are permitted to purchase from abroad.

Benny went to New York with Dennis to look for locations for the first show. While he was there he was invited to present an Emmy Award to British comedian Alexei Sayle, whom he admired, so he agreed without hesitation. He was quite enchanted with the whole glittering occasion, impressed that one of his screen heroines, Audrey Hepburn, had been there.

'They gave me two Penthouse Pets to take me down the staircase in case I fell,' he enthused, 'and you should have seen the limousine I had to take me around everywhere. It was like a boat on wheels, vast expanses of shining leather inside, and me sitting in the back with a girl on either side.' Back home the British papers were still doing stories about him travelling everywhere by bus. 'So there I was in the back of this stretch limo with a bottle of champagne in one hand and a glass in the other,' he said, 'and I thought to myself, "I wonder what number bus this is?"'

While he was in New York he asked if he could possibly meet flamboyant property millionaire Donald Trump, who fascinated him. Don Taffner said: 'Our publicity lady fixed it easily, because Donald Trump quite likes having his photo taken. But they were going up the Trump Tower in a crowded lift and it was Benny who was getting all the attention. I don't think Donald liked that quite so much.'

Benny had been asked to give the first show some real American references, including a sketch about the TV agony aunt, Dr Ruth. He had a plan to write Donald Trump into a quickie too. 'I drop a coin as I run past him outside the Trump Tower, and he looks round furtively and then puts it in his pocket.' It was one of many plans that never came to fruition. But the Americans had made more fuss of him on that trip than ever before, and it boosted his morale at just the right psychological moment.

His sacking was somehow making him more gregarious, more inclined to accept the invitations which earlier would have gone straight into the waste-paper basket. Perhaps he now wanted people to see that he was still alive, still in business.

For years he had refused every request for a TV chat show, whether it was Parkinson, or Wogan. He was terrified of being caught off guard. But now he agreed to appear on a Dutch chat show, provided the ever-faithful Kirkland could be on it too, to protect him from anything he didn't want to answer. The pair did their well-rehearsed double act and Benny found to his astonishment that it was quite painless. No one was trying to put him on the spot.

So he did one in New York and was thrilled that his audience for his appearance shot up to three times what it had been for the previous show. He did another TV show in Spain, started giving far more press interviews than ever before, and accepted an invitation to be photographed with the glamorous girls from the Crazy Horse saloon in Paris. 'I said, oh no, I wish you wouldn't do this. I protested ... honestly!' he insisted. 'But I think I'm going to do more personal appearances in future. They're quite fun.'

It was arranged that he would return to New York to film the local inserts in the spring. Meanwhile, there was the question of where they would make the rest of the show. The obvious answer, extraordinarily, was at Thames' studios, which would be rented out to the Taffner organization as a facilities house. Dennis Kirkland would also go back as director, but they would use Thames make-up, costumes, props and technical crews. Thames also agreed to sell Taffner some left-over footage from the last batch of location filming. It would be almost like old times.

Everyone assumed Benny would be reluctant to return

to the scene of his humiliation, but he was practical as ever. It was nearby, it was convenient, and all his costumes and props were there. He told me he had no qualms about going back. Instead he was looking forward to seeing all his old friends. 'After all, I don't have any quarrel with any of them.' It was fixed for January 1990.

He spent Christmas 1989 on his own as usual, watching television and taping everything he couldn't watch. One of Thames' Christmas Day programmes was a compilation of the company's twenty-year comedy output, introduced by Jim Davidson. It included a clip of Benny. Someone, somewhere at Thames, still loved him, he decided. He went to Bournemouth to see Louise English in panto, and took all the Little Angels for their usual Christmas treat.

For his sixty-sixth birthday a few weeks later, he had a magnum of champagne from Thames, too. But it came from staff at the Thames TV International office, who were still selling old editions of 'The Benny Hill Show', and were still grateful to him.

I phoned him the day before his birthday, and for the first time in many years he had no plans for a celebration with 'the family'. His birthday fell on a Sunday so none of them would be around. 'I shall be doing virtually nothing,' he said rather forlornly. 'I have got to get on and do some alterations to the script, and do some rehearsing on my own. I must practise my monologues and songs. So it will be almost like an ordinary day.'

Rehearsals were due to start the following Wednesday so people were not far away, but Benny wouldn't have dreamed of asking them to join him on a non-working day, even for a party. 'Some of them would have to come quite a distance,' he pointed out. 'To ask them in specially would be a bit much.'

The American special was duly made and screened on the USA Cable Network. But plans for the rest of the series gradually foundered. The recession had hit the TV industry worldwide, and while foreign stations were happy to buy 'The Benny Hill Show' as a completed package, putting the money up-front to make it was a different matter.

He had two years of virtual inactivity while waiting for something to happen, but he never gave up hope that it would. Meanwhile, he accepted more invitations from America. One of his favourite trips, which he did more than once, was to be a judge at the Miss Hawaiian Tropic beauty pageant. It was the sort of event which was no longer acceptable in Britain. Even the Miss World contest had been dropped from national television. But this small triumph for the Women's Lib movement had totally passed Benny by, along with all the other feminist break-throughs. He still thought beauty contests were a small patch of heaven on earth.

Back home he started dividing his time almost equally between Teddington and Southampton, usually spending alternate fortnights in each. In Southampton, he dis-covered a small private chauffeur company run by David Goodall, and started riding around in more style than usual in a Volvo 714, with a uniformed David in the driving seat. Stylish it may have been, but it was also far cheaper than any other chauffeur service he had ever used before, he told David. 'It wasn't that he didn't like spending money,' said David, 'but he wouldn't exactly go looking for things to spend it on.'

Instead of walking to Tesco or Sainsbury with his carr-iers, he now went by car. 'But he was very funny,' said David. 'He would tell me to wait in Tesco's car park, then I would see him go in the back door of the store and out the front, going somewhere else he didn't want to tell me about.'

Benny would claim that he didn't want pomp and circumstance when he went out and merely wanted to blend in with the crowd. But if he and David went in a pub or café during one of their outings, he had the driver keep his cap and gloves on, which automatically attracted a bit of notice. 'I could never work out whether he wanted attention or whether he didn't. He was very deep,' said David. Benny would regularly send him to the bank to pick up small amounts of cash for him, £150 or £200, but even so he would always run out. 'We'd be picking up his laundry and dry cleaning, and suddenly it would be, "Oh dear, lend me a tenner, David." '

Goodall was frequently hired to drive Benny up to London and back. Sometimes he spent the journey deep in thought, or scribbling on bits of paper. Other times he was chatty and curious about his driver's life. He kept saying he was going to call round for tea to see David's two dogs, a Rottweiler and a Jack Russell, but he never did.

If Dennis Kirkland was in the car, Benny would be altogether different again, giggling like a schoolboy. 'Sometimes I had trouble keeping my eyes on the road, they'd be making me laugh so much,' David said. Dennis was doing a sterling job of keeping Benny's spirits up, devoting himself to the task practically full-time.

David asked for the phone number of Benny's flat in Teddington several times so that he could check various pick-up arrangements with him, but Benny went all secretive and pretended he couldn't remember it. And though David went to Westrow Gardens many times, he was never allowed over the threshold. Benny would often have difficulty opening the door, because the hall floor was just a carpet of unopened mail. 'He would have to kick it aside with his foot to get the door back, sort of shuffle it to one side.' Considering how much mail there was, it was a miracle it got read, but it must have done because Benny always paid his bills by return of post, and always responded to every request for a signed photograph. David added: 'I couldn't see anything inside the house for him to be embarrassed by, it was just a bit old-fashioned, but he wouldn't let me in. One day I asked to use the bathroom and he told me to follow him, came out of the front door, round the garden at the side, and into a little lobby by the back door. There was a toilet there.'

Benny didn't always travel by chauffeur-driven car. He still went off for lengthy walks. He particularly liked the cathedral towns around the area, Winchester and Salisbury, travelling there by train. And of course, he still shuttled backwards and forwards to the Isle of Wight.

He would turn up unannounced at the Whittakers', or phone Sylvia Thorley and ask her to invite a few girls over for him to take to lunch. He no longer had the excuse of auditioning girls for the show, so his dates were purely social. But there was no question of romance. He just revelled in the company of the very young and attractive. 'He'd say, "Just invite a few nice young ladies". He liked girls who were not too spoiled or sophisticated, who would appreciate being treated to nice meals at smart restaurants,' said Sylvia. Nothing had changed.

Mimi made the mistake one day of inviting him to be guest of honour at a Water Rats charity function. Benny quickly declined. As ever, it wasn't the done thing to presume on his friendship. The initiative had to come from him. When Sylvia mentioned one day that Billy and

Mimi were running tea-dances at Ryde Pavilion, almost like those he had attended on the pier nearly sixty years before, he immediately asked if he could go to one.

When he walked in, said Mimi, it was like the opening credits of 'Dr Kildare'. All the dancers froze in mid-step as they saw who was coming into the room. Benny drew the line at dancing, but he helped organize the raffle, folding up the tickets and putting them in the bucket before he drew out the winners.

Despite these frequent visits to the Isle of Wight, he never once called on his agent, Richard Stone, who now had a home on the island, just as he had not looked up his old friend Bob Monkhouse when Bob was doing a summer season in Ryde. Instead he sent a card to Philip Jones saying: 'I arrived here just after the Bob Monkhouse show closed. Now where am I going to get some jokes for my new series?' In fact, staff at the theatre thought they had seen Benny in the audience. But he did not come round to the stagedoor to see Bob.

He took Sylvia Thorley for numerous lobster salads and cream teas, and attended several parties at her home. One day one of her clients was there with her elderly mother. The pair politely lurked upstairs, knowing that Benny did not like friends and neighbours being wheeled in to stare at him. Benny spotted the old lady at a window. 'Come on down,' he shouted. 'Will you marry me? I bet you'll say yes. None of the others did. They all turned me down.'

Back in Southampton, he was a regular visitor to another old lady, Mimi Levy, supplier of his favourite meringues, who was now nearly ninety. She had a friend who used to take her out in a little caravanette, and Benny would join them on their expeditions, pottering round the countryside. It was an average sort of life for any other senior citizen but not for one of the 200 richest men in Britain.

Without a show definitely scheduled, Benny now had no incentive to diet and his eating was beginning to get out of hand. He had discovered a new restaurant, Browns Brasserie, not far from Westrow Gardens.

Owner Richard Brown remembers the first time Benny went there. 'I was inside cleaning the chrome-work,' he said, 'when I noticed this figure sitting outside, surrounded by carrier bags. I thought at first it was some sort of hobo.' The he recognized Benny and went outside to speak to him. Benny wasn't sure if the place was open or not, and was waiting for some sign. He had a pile of newspapers, television magazines and children's comics under his arm.

From then on, Benny went to Browns quite regularly. He always had a full three-course meal and followed it by eating all the home-made petits fours served with the coffee. 'I always gave him a good selection and he always ate the lot,' said Richard. 'His problem was he liked all the rich things.'

Sometimes he would go to the restaurant on his own, more often with several girls. He would phone David Goodall and ask him to pick him up and take him to Browns, adding: 'I may need you to pick up someone else as well.'

'He always knew very well that he'd invited a couple of girls he wanted me to collect,' said David. 'Always young, in their twenties. Afterwards I'd pick them up from the restaurant and take them to one of the late-night clubs at the Marina for more drinks.'

It would be the small hours before they emerged. Benny would sit in the middle with a girl on either side, and there'd be shrieks and screams of laughter. 'We had some

very noisy nights,' said David. But the car always went
to Westrow Gardens first. His two giggling companions
would peck him on the cheek, he'd be dropped off, and
then the girls would be driven home.

19

Rehabilitation

Benny's 1990 Christmas was much the same as his others, except for one special outing. He organized 'Uncle Ben's Panto Party', but this time for the Whittakers and Sylvia Thorley and her husband. They were invited to the Mayflower Theatre in Southampton, to see Cannon and Ball in *Babes in the Wood*. Unfortunately, Billy was unwell and couldn't go. The others were treated to a sumptuous lunch at a hotel, then ate ice-creams throughout the matinée. Afterwards they called at several other cafés and bars for more food and drink. 'The wine never stopped flowing,' said Mimi. 'We even had one last bottle of wine as we got back on the ferry home.'

A few days later Benny phoned me. The Broadcasting Standards Council was due to begin official operation in the first week of January 1991, and it was still very much on Benny's mind. 'Are you writing anything about the BSC?' he demanded. I was in the middle of cooking and he caught me on the hop. 'The BSC?' I said, racking my brains as to why I might be writing about the British Safety Council, or whatever those initials stood for.

'Call yourself a journalist!' said Benny impatiently. 'The Broadcasting Standards Council! Because if you are, this is what you should say.' He then delivered a twenty-minute lecture on the double standards in television, and what other comedians and drama producers were getting away with, compared to his own alleged offences.

In the event, the BSC turned out to be far more liberal than many people had anticipated. For instance, in the twelve months between April 1991 and March 1992, the Council received 1,130 complaints on matters which it considered to be within its remit, and reached formal findings on 627 of them. Out of these, 117 were upheld or partly upheld. The large majority of the items complained about was declared by the council to be 'unlikely to cause widespread offence'. I used to pass some of the Council's monthly reports on to Benny, and he was intrigued to read its solemn adjudications. Would 'The Benny Hill Show' have been deemed 'likely to cause widespread offence'?

He was coming further and further out of his shell. In 1991, he allowed the first ever documentary to be made about him, for the BBC's prestigious arts series, 'Omnibus'. He had met producer Victor Pemberton and director David Spencer at the Emmy Awards in New York a couple of years earlier when they had received an award for their profile of the actress Gwen Ffrangcon-Davies. Benny remembered seeing the film and liking it so much he made a mental note of the independent production company responsible, Saffron.

Now Saffron suggested that they make a film about him. 'He lowered his eyes shyly and said, "Oh I'll have to think about it,"' said Victor. It took a couple of years for Benny to agree. Things moved along a little faster when he and Pemberton discovered an immediate rapport. As a schoolboy, Victor had seen Benny live at the Finsbury Park Empire. Victor could also list dozens of other music-hall acts, some of which even Benny didn't remember. They had lots to talk about.

Getting ready for a scene with the girls, on location in Thorpe
Park, Surrey, in 1987.

Momentarily unrecognized in a New York café, where Benny
took the author to lunch in March 1987.

Letting his hair down at one of Sylvia Thorley's parties in 1989 (*Celia Niemiec, Sandown, Isle of Wight*).

Fairwater House, Teddington, Benny's final home.

Benny at home in Fairwater House, watching TV as usual (*Scope Features*).

However, the final decision wasn't made until they had taken him out to lunch at L'Etoile in Charlotte Street. As soon as he got inside the restaurant and he realized this was going to be an expensive lunch for the pair, he put his cards on the table. He told them there was something they should know. He'd had an offer from another film company for a documentary. 'So if you don't want to pay for lunch I'll quite understand,' he said. But the lunch went ahead anyway, and by the end of it the project was virtually agreed. He said yes officially a couple of days later.

He was still nervous, though. The ways of documentary making were strange to him and if he had had his way, the whole thing would have been scripted and rehearsed. It started badly when they set up the very first shot in Vevey, Switzerland.

Benny had been invited by Charlie Chaplin's son Eugene to chair the jury at the eighteenth Vevey comedy festival and to receive a special Charlie Chaplin Award for services to comedy. As Benny got out of his car, the cameras turned and Victor Pemberton called out: 'How does it feel to be in Vevey?' Benny's face clouded. He stopped the cameras and said: 'No, no, no, I don't think that's a good idea.'

Pemberton swiftly realized that Benny could not cope with anything impromptu, however innocuous. He had to know exactly what was happening and what would be said. In Paris, the same thing happened when a French TV news crew got into a reception given for Benny at the British Embassy.

Saffron had decided to take Benny to France to film him walking down the Champs-Elysées and meeting his French public. But someone in the BBC office in Paris thought it would be even better if they could lay on some

sort of party for him. Starting at the top, she contacted
the British Ambassador, Sir Ewan Ferguson, who turned
out to be a fervent Benny Hill fan. He was delighted not
only to host a huge reception for Benny but to appear in
the film proclaiming that he and his whole family were
avid viewers of 'The Benny Hill Show'.

There was a slight contretemps when about forty of the
French press were locked outside and started trying very
rowdily to get in. A French TV crew wanted to show
Benny live on the news that night, but Benny would not
go along with the idea of appearing live at all. 'He just
couldn't take anything unscripted,' said Pemberton. In
the end a compromise was reached and he pre-recorded
a small item to be shown later.

There was also the problem of Benny insisting on bringing Dennis Kirkland along with him as a sort of security
blanket. There is nothing a producer and director want
less than another producer/director unofficially super-
vising their efforts. 'Kirkland was everywhere, morning,
noon and night,' says Pemberton. 'It was a very difficult
relationship for everyone to cope with. But we tried to
understand, and we soon learned that Benny needed him
there for confidence. He had to have him around.'

Once these problems were ironed out, the whole experience was a sheer delight. They filmed for about twelve
months on and off, in London and Southampton as well
as Paris and Vevey. Benny obviously enjoyed the filming
because it was almost like being back at work again and
he never stopped trying to make everyone laugh.

In Teddington Victor and David were frequent and
welcome visitors to the flat, despite the untidiness and
the half-eaten takeaways. After filming they would take
him back to Fairwater House and discover that Benny
had got a couple of bottles of champagne on ice, even

though Victor does not drink. He never wanted them to leave. It was often two or three in the morning before they got away.

At Westrow Gardens, like everyone else, they barely got over the doorstep. Once they asked to use the loo, and as he had done with David Goodall, Benny took them round through the garden to the toilet at the back of the house. Much as they would have liked to look inside, they were never invited into the living-room. He told them repeatedly about his plans to decorate: he was going to have the whole house done up and get new furniture. 'But I never saw any sign of it being done,' said Pemberton.

Benny had apparently had the bathroom redone, and told me very proudly about the gold taps. Then he hastily corrected himself: 'I just mean gold-coloured. They're not real gold.' I hadn't imagined they would be. There was a rumour that the plumber had found little notes everywhere saying, 'Don't touch this' and 'Don't touch that'.

Benny kept telling everyone he was going to buy a flat of his own in London. He even claimed that there was a particular one on the river he had his eye on, but no one really believed any of it. 'It just sounded like a story he had been telling people for years,' said Pemberton.

Before the 'Omnibus' programme was shown, Benny made another small breakthrough, and appeared on Des O'Connor's popular Thames TV show. It was actually Benny's first chat show on British TV, though to be fair, it is far more rehearsed and scripted than other chat shows. You may not have thought so on the infamous occasion when Des lost control of two of his guests, comic Stan Boardman and actor Oliver Reed, but with Benny the whole thing was worked out between the two professionals beforehand.

Benny enjoyed it so much he agreed to go back in the autumn of 1992 and do an hour's conversational special, featuring just him and Des. Meanwhile, he could not resist a little joke at Victor Pemberton's expense. He came on as Fred Scuttle and announced that he was an independent TV producer. 'What does an independent producer do?' asked Des, on cue. 'Absolutely nothing at all,' gurgled Benny.

His money continued to fascinate people. In December he was asked by an interviewer if he had made a will, and admitted that his only will left everything to his parents, who had of course predeceased him. So he must make a new one, he said.

He was asked who would figure in it. For instance, would Phoebe King and Netta Warner be on the list? Certainly, said Benny. Would they be at the top of the list? Yes, said Benny obligingly. This in itself does not mean much. Many wills deal with the small bequests first before disposing of the bulk of the estate.

The paper chose to interpret it as Benny confirming that Netta and Phoebe would be the main beneficiaries in his new will. Mrs Garrison, warden at Phoebe's housing complex, was anxious enough about the implications to mention it to Benny next time she spoke to him. 'You mustn't believe everything you read in the papers,' he told her. But the impression persisted that Phoebe and Netta were to be his heirs. It was to cause a lot of heartache later on.

He spoke to many people about his will over the next few weeks, giving several of them the firm idea that he actually had made a new one. David Goodall said: 'He definitely told me he had just made a will. We were talking about money and the cost of things, and he was in a serious mood. It was not a joke.' Richard Stone thinks

Benny probably had every intention of making one, but simply didn't get round to it.

When the 'Omnibus' programme was screened on 20 December people who hadn't seen Benny for a while were shocked at how fat and puffy he looked. The Saffron team say his health seemed fine during the months of filming, but they were taken aback by his prodigious eating and drinking. 'We suspected something would happen quite dramatically,' said Pemberton. 'His weight was just going up and up, he ate enormously.'

As they were getting ready to leave one restaurant in Paris, Benny cleared the table. 'He ate everything people had left on their plates and drained all their glasses. It was a bit terrifying. We tried to watch him, but what could I say when I was eating ice-cream cones all the time myself? So the two of us would be licking our ice-creams.'

'Omnibus' was a genuinely heartfelt tribute to Benny's artistry and popularity, and boosted his spirits enormously. If ever there was a time for a comeback this was it. And attempts to get his real career back on the tracks were continuing apace.

In October 1991, under a new system invented by Margaret Thatcher's government, Thames TV had lost their franchise to broadcast in the London area. Franchises were awarded to the highest bidder unless 'exceptional circumstances' were invoked. No exceptional circumstances were claimed for Thames and the valuable franchise went to a new consortium, Carlton Television. Several friends phoned Benny to say: 'It serves Thames right, doesn't it?'

Benny was having none of it. It was no cause for rejoicing, he rebuked them. Lots of old friends would lose their jobs. 'And after all, I had twenty-one very happy years there.'

Once Thames had got over the shock, the company courageously picked itself up, dusted itself down and prepared to become an independent production company. Thames would in future sell shows to other ITV companies or to the BBC or wherever there was a market. It did not take them long to realize that some new Benny Hill shows would be a strong item in a package of programmes, both abroad where the demand for Benny was as strong as ever, and at home, where the climate of opinion about him was slowly changing.

First Dennis Kirkland was brought back to re-edit some previous shows into half-hour compilations for screening in spring 1992, as a way of re-educating the audience. Political correctness was apparently out. Then Benny was invited to lunch by John Fisher, John Howard Davies' deputy, to discuss whether he would like to return to his old stamping ground to make one hour-long show, with the possibility of more.

Meanwhile, on 22 August, the indefatigable Philip Jones had written to Andy Allen, an old Thames colleague who was now programme boss of Central Television. He pointed out that 'one of our greatest comics' had been off the air for two years, and suggested it would be a good idea for Central to pick up the show.

'Bless him,' said Philip, 'he rang me straight away. He responded positively, promptly, professionally and helpfully.' And things started to move through the pipeline. Even the incoming company, Carlton, had expressed an interest.

When I met Benny for lunch just before Christmas he told me he was considering several offers. To my shame, I did not think anything would come of them. After all, two and a half years had gone by without anything happening. I thought they were all just straws for him to clutch at, and feared he would be disappointed once again. He was nearly sixty-eight, and at last beginning to look it. For the first time, I noticed a couple of wrinkles in that smooth, plump face. Was it really time to start a whole new career?

He was indignant. The idea of retirement was anathema to him. A life of leisure held no attraction. 'What else is there to think about except work?' he asked. 'If you've got a brain that's constantly looking for ideas, you can't just stop it working. Someone said to me, "You don't need to work, you could just lie on a beach all day." But you've still got to think about something, even lying on a beach.' He was absolutely convinced he would work again: 'Oh yes, definitely.'

He ate a lot that lunchtime but he seemed as fit as ever. He was full, as usual, of plans to have more work done at Westrow Gardens. He admitted that he could no longer live with his mother's old kitchen equipment. He had realized at last just how ancient and inefficient it was. The gas stove had been there since the thirties, and you had to strike match after match before it would light.

'It all looks so awful, I can't invite any young ladies back there just yet,' he said, buffing up his image to the end. By now, according to Chris Hill, Benny actually *had* done something about the house instead of just talking about it. Roger Whatling had started the work. 'It definitely looked a bit better,' said Chris.

The previous day, he told me, he had taken a train from Teddington to Putney, then walked all the way from Putney to St John's Wood to his dentist. On the way he had called in at Harrods to look at furniture. He had decided that his old furniture seemed dated and heavy against the new red and gold wallpaper, so he had to choose some replacements. But he had been mesmerized by the sheer choice in the vast department, and resolved to go back again taking Sue Upton with him to give him some advice.

He was still working on script ideas. He had just seen the film of *Cyrano de Bergerac*, starring Gerard Depardieu. 'You know him, of course,' he said. 'He's so famous he has his own room set aside at every airport in the world. It's called the Depardieu Lounge.' Ouch! He had worked out a whole sketch based on a send-up of the Cyrano story and it is to be hoped that the other jokes were better.

When we came out of the restaurant I offered him a lift back to the flat, but he said he would walk and do some shopping on his way home. He kissed me full on the lips instead of his usual showbiz peck on the cheek, and strode briskly down Teddington High Street. It was the last time I saw him.

20

The Final Weeks

Benny spent his last Christmas at home in Southampton, watching TV as usual, and eating a heat-and-serve meal. On Christmas Eve, his old school pal, John Spencer, was visiting another friend in Westrow Gardens and decided to knock on Benny's door. He hadn't seen or spoken to him for years. Benny's voice called out: 'Who's there?' John bent to the letter box and identified himself. Benny, reluctant as ever to let anyone in, called back: 'I can't come to the door at the moment.' So John pushed a note through with his address and phone number. On Christmas Day, in between essential TV viewing, Benny decided to call him. They chatted about old times for over an hour.

On New Year's Eve, he was in party mood. David Goodall drove him to the home of wealthy friends near Petersfield. He was asked to wait outside till Benny was ready to go home. But just after midnight, Benny came out and said he was enjoying himself so much, he would stay the night and David could come back for him the following lunchtime. It was most unusual for him not to want to sleep in his own bed.

The next day David returned and found the house empty. After about an hour, Benny turned up with his hosts. They had decided to start 1992 with a nice healthy walk.

For once, Benny did not celebrate his birthday with colleagues from the show. Instead he went to Browns Restaurant with a friend who kept a theatrical boarding house in Southampton, plus six of the girls who were appearing in the local panto. When the ratio of men to women was stacked in his favour like that, he was the life and soul of the party, and this was no exception.

He was still eating and drinking huge amounts, and rounded off the meal with his usual petits-fours, even though at this point he knew there was a strong possibility of being back in front of the cameras quite soon. But he could not bring himself to diet just yet.

A few weeks earlier he had met up with some old school friends, a married couple, and was astonished to learn that they lived just round the corner. 'If only I'd known,' he cried. The husband suffered from multiple sclerosis, and Benny had determined to keep in touch with them from now on. He told them: 'I'm good at pushing a wheelchair.' On 30 January he visited them at their home and they laughed and chatted all day, though Benny declined to have any food. He was going to a party that night and saving himself, he said. But they arranged to see him again after Easter together with some other old friends.

At his home in Maidenhead, Jon Jon Keefe was still waiting for the show to get back on the road. If finance was the problem, he couldn't understand why Benny didn't just use his own money to set up an independent production. He had enough of it. Since this seemed unlikely to happen, Jon Jon had tried to start things moving himself. His wife had met someone at a local car boot sale whose son-in-law was in the film business. Through this unlikely route, Jon Jon made contact with someone else in the TV and film financing business who might be able to raise enough cash, and got a meeting set up for Dennis Kirkland at the Meridien Hotel in Piccadilly. But it turned out that the independent financing wouldn't be necessary after all.

The Central deal was bubbling along nicely. The company had seen the American show Benny had made, and were not too impressed with it, but they appreciated the reasons why it had been given such an American flavour. Now they wanted Benny to dream up some brand-new characters to augment his repertoire of old favourites like Fred Scuttle, and give the shows a fresh feel for the nineties. This he was more than willing to do.

At first, Benny was inclined to accept John Fisher's Thames offer. Pragmatic as ever, he thought it would be more handy to get to work from the flat, and all his old costumes and props, including Fred Scuttle's specs, were after all still at Thames, though it is doubtful if some of the costumes would have fitted him the way he had blown up.

Jon Jon Keefe was amazed. 'We were all vindictive towards Thames on his behalf. I mean, if it happened to you, wouldn't you make sure that you never dealt with them again? But he may have wanted to prove a point by going back to do the show from there again. And of course he felt secure, knowing everybody in wardrobe and make-up and all the other faces. But frankly it was the last place most of us would have wanted to go back to because of what they had done.'

Richard Stone had retired from the day-to-day running of the agency though he was still its *éminence grise*. Lynda Ronan, who had taken over as Benny's agent, consulted with Richard, who advised against accepting Thames' offer. He thought it would be quite ignominious to go back to Thames, he said. They had lost their franchise and were just looking for product so that they could sell a package deal to one of the other ITV companies. It would be much better to go direct to one of the companies which had retained its franchise to broadcast.

Stone also spoke to Benny and told him the same thing. The Central deal was the one to take. Benny went along with the decision. He still respected Richard's instincts.

Now they negotiated with Central over where the show should be made – Benny was not keen to go to Nottingham where Central Productions was based. A compromise was worked out that he could do the outdoor filming in the London area, and the studio recording and editing in Nottingham. He was very keen to be involved in the editing as usual, a situation Central was not accustomed to with any of its other artists, but was willing to accommodate.

Benny agreed that he would stay in a hotel in Nottingham whenever he was needed, and lined up David Goodall to drive him backwards and forwards. The best part of the deal was that Central had agreed to a huge budget, up to £510,000 per hour, so the show would have the same lavish look as the Thames productions. He would be able to work the way he loved to work.

Meanwhile, he suddenly found himself going to a lot of funerals. A few months earlier, he had attended Mimi Levy's at Southampton's Hollybrook Cemetery. Afterwards, he walked a friend across to his parents' grave and told her, 'That's where I'm going to be buried.' He always took flowers to the grave whenever he was in Westrow Gardens, walking the six miles there and back. The cemetery staff knew him as a very shy, sweet man. When he was in London, his friend replaced the dead flowers with fresh ones.

Then in November, he went to the funeral of Jack Breckon, Thames' former picture publicity editor, in Kent. That was the day when Benny discovered en route that he had no cuff-links. He and Kirkland, already late for the service, stopped at a store, threw some money on the counter and grabbed the cuff-links without waiting for them to be wrapped. A zealous security officer stopped them on suspicion of shoplifting! It made headlines in the *News of the World*.

He and Dennis attended Jack's memorial service, held at the journalists' church, St Bride's in Fleet Street, on 5 February. David Goodall drove them, and found Benny was in exceptionally high spirits, laughing all the way. 'They were being outrageous,' he said. Benny had planned to leave at the end of the service, and drive straight to Southampton, but in the end, he decided to attend the reception afterwards instead. Everyone thought he looked fine.

Two days later, on 7 February, there was another funeral. Ted Taylor had been Thames' rehearsal pianist, a much-loved man who had a sticker on his piano saying: If at first you don't succeed, lower your standards. His widow had decided to give him a splendid send-off with a post-funeral party in a marquee. Benny met many old friends there, including his former backing group, The Ladybirds. 'The place was throbbing,' said Jon Jon Keefe. 'In the church, Benny had looked terribly, terribly sad, but afterwards he had a great time. He and Kirkland had to pour themselves out of there.'

By now Benny was already beginning to get chest pains, especially at night. He told Dennis Kirkland about them, and Dennis tried to reassure him that it was probably indigestion. With Benny's triumphant return to British television so very nearly in the bag neither of them wanted to face up to the fact that it could be something worse.

During yet another business meeting on Sunday 9 February, Benny started getting pains again. He told Kirkland: 'I really don't think it can be indigestion this time.' He called his doctor and on Monday 10 February, he was admitted to the private Cromwell Hospital where he had last been because of his ulcer eight years earlier.

At first, he tried to pretend he had just gone in for tests for an insurance medical, but in fact it was a mild heart attack. Kirkland had now taken on the role of press agent in addition to producer, friend, unofficial manager and minder. A series of merry quips issued from the hospital supposedly from Benny's lips but they had mostly been made up by Kirkland.

Benny was not at all well. Few calls were being put through, but he insisted on speaking to Sue Upton, and when Louise English rang, she told staff she was like a daughter to him and should be treated as family, so she managed to get a few words. His cousin Chris had a terrible job to get through. 'They seemed to think I was a reporter. In the end I got hold of a Sister who remembered me going to visit him when he had his ulcer, so I managed to speak to him at last.'

On 18 February, Benny left the Cromwell but had breathing problems almost immediately and later that night was admitted to the Royal Brompton National Heart and Lung Hospital in Chelsea, a National Health Service hospital with some private rooms. Despite being really ill this time, Benny insisted on visiting a young patient awaiting a heart and lung transplant. The hospital authorities were touched by his gesture and say it did wonders for the child's morale. As Kirkland held press conferences on the hospital steps, Annette André was among those who managed to get through to Benny on the phone. He also heard the sad news that Netta Warner had died.

On 22 February, Benny received a bizarre visit from the singer Michael Jackson who was staying in London. Benny was bemused by the whole episode. He was not really well enough for all the fuss the visit involved. Slender American superstar, flanked by minders, sat and regarded plump British superstar, sitting up in bed in his pyjamas. It was hardly a meeting of minds: Jackson's every gesture was a totally calculated piece of media manipulation, while Benny's interest in publicity was minimal. The main thing they had in common, possibly, was their apparent self-sufficiency, their reputation for being loners, able to live happily with their own company regardless of what people thought.

Jackson, however, was a self-declared fan, and told Benny how he thought he was greater than Chaplin. They chatted about working together when Benny was better. Perhaps he could appear in Michael's next video.

Meanwhile, he starred in another video. Richard Stone was due to celebrate his golden wedding anniversary in April, and his two sons were asking all his clients to make a home video of themselves to be secretly edited together into a congratulatory tape for Richard and Sara. Lynda Ronan took a camcorder to the Brompton and filmed Benny. He ruffled up his hair, and slumped down in the bed. He was wearing a hospital gown and had electrodes stuck to his skin. In a quavering voice he congratulated Richard and Sara on their anniversary.

Then he sat up, looking perfectly well, and pretended to think the recording had ended. 'Are we off? Good, let's have some champagne.' Resurrecting his old joke from forty years earlier, he added confidentially: 'Nice woman, that Sara Stone. She won't come up, you know, but a nice woman.' Then he demanded several bottles of champagne to toast the happy couple.

Lynda said: 'He was fine when we made that tape. The way he looked at the beginning was all put on, and after I'd stopped filming we carried on talking and laughing for about an hour.' But when I telephoned him on the day he was supposed to go home, he was trying to pack his own things together and sounded breathless and far from his normal self.

Benny had developed fluid in his lungs. The drugs normally used to rid the body of surplus fluid had to be carefully controlled because Benny had only one kidney, so it took a while to find the correct dosage. When Louise English phoned, he told her he felt as if he was drowning in his own body. They had a long conversation and though he was struggling for breath and had to pause between sentences, he was determined to say what he had to say. 'He seemed to have a lot he wanted to get across.'

Benny had just agreed to be a guest on 'Desert Island Discs'. Through Dennis, he issued a joke about deciding to do it because host Sue Lawley had the best legs in showbusiness. He may not have fully appreciated her penetrative interviewing style, which lets few castaways escape from the island without a bout of self-examination. But thinking up his eight records gave him something to do in hospital.

He asked Louise if she had a recording of herself singing Ivor Novello's *Glamorous Nights*, which he wanted as one of his eight. He explained: 'I have two very happy memories of that song. When I was a soldier in the war, I used to listen to the words and it made me think of my mother. And the second is when I came to see you at the Mill Theatre in Sonning.'

Despite being so breathless, Benny reminisced for a long time about the day at Sonning, going for the meal in Marlow and walking round the shops afterwards. 'It was one of the best days of my life,' he told her.

Louise said: 'He sounded very ill, and must have known how ill he was because he was very sentimental. Every time he said something really sentimental I waited for him to lighten it with a funny punchline like he usually did. But it never came.'

He told her he wanted to be there when she took over as Sally in the hit musical *Me and My Girl* at the Adelphi Theatre on 9 March. He did not normally attend her first nights, knowing she would have all her family there, but this time was different, he said. 'I'm going to bring everyone I know to see you, and tell them, "That's how it should be done," ' he informed her. She waited for his usual pay off: 'So now will you practise!' But it didn't come. When opening night arrived, he was too ill to attend, but he still desperately wanted to see the show.

Benny went home on 24 February, but was re-admitted a few weeks later with the same breathing problem. He was discharged again on 31 March, with strict instructions to lose about two stone. He was well over seventeen stone at this point. He really wasn't well enough to go straight home to an empty flat and fend for himself. Friends told him he needed a nurse or companion to move in and look after him, but that was anathema. His desire for privacy was really to be the death of him.

The deal with Central was now nearly home and dry. The company was worried about Benny's health, but they had been assured that the problem was negligible and he just needed to rest and lose weight. He was pictured in a newspaper using an exercise bicycle, but it was just for the photographs.

Just after he got home, Phoebe King had a fall and broke her femur. Brenda Garrison rang Benny to tell him. He wanted to know what he could do to help. His first thought was to go out and order flowers. 'But I'm not supposed to walk more than twelve steps without someone to help me,' he said anxiously.

Nevertheless he did manage to send flowers, and he rang the hospital where Phoebe was waiting for an operation. She had already told the staff that Benny Hill was her friend, but they didn't really believe her until the phone call. He told Phoebe: 'We are a pair, aren't we, my darling?' When she moved to a convalescent home after leaving hospital, more bouquets of flowers arrived.

In April, the Central deal was finalized at last. The plan was to do two shows, with an option on a third. Filming would start in August. The shows would be directed by Dennis Kirkland and produced by Central's new controller of entertainment, Richard Holloway, who had known Dennis since they began their TV careers together at ATV Elstree. The ITV schedule for Christmas 1992 was already being drawn up and the two shows were slotted into prime positions over the Christmas holiday.

Meanwhile, Central booked a hotel in Switzerland for a press lunch during the Montreux TV Festival, due to start on 26 April. There they would make a formal announcement of the contract. Holloway was tremendously excited by his coup and couldn't wait to start work.

In mid-April, Benny rang his cousin Chris and said he wouldn't be coming to Southampton in the foreseeable future. 'It bothers me now, but at the time it seemed innocent enough. He said he thought he was going to stay in Teddington for the time being because he didn't want to get too far away from the hospital. I can't help wondering now if he knew something that we didn't.'

Benny had kept asking Louise English when he could come to *Me and My Girl*. She suggested he wait till he felt better, but he was adamant that it was urgent. It was fixed for the matinée of Wednesday 15 April. On 14 April, Sylvia Thorley rang to ask if he'd like to go down to Southsea to see a show about the life of George Formby. Benny said: 'I'm not well enough to be up to that, I'm afraid. But guess where I'm going tomorrow!'

It had been arranged that he would be collected by taxi and meet Sue Upton and another old friend, Samantha Spencer-Lane, for lunch at the Savoy before the matinée. Louise would not join them because Benny knew she would be too nervous. Benny had also asked her if she could arrange for some press pictures to be taken of his trip to the theatre. She was puzzled because he usually liked to make his theatre visits incognito, but this time he was insistent, so she fixed it with the show's publicists.

Throughout the performance, she could see his face beaming proudly in the stalls. After the show, the stage lights were left on for a few minutes for the picture session. Benny came up for what would prove to be his last appearance on a stage, and posed wearing a bowler hat with Louise and her co-star Les Dennis. She still doesn't know why Benny was so keen on the pictures. Did he have some premonition and want to leave her the legacy of the final photographs? Or did he want the outside world to see that he was up and about again, and feeling fine? Afterwards, he went round to Louise's dressing-room. He met as many people as could crowd into it, chatted to another cast member, Alfred Marks, about the old days when they had done a radio show together, and generally had a whale of a time.

When the others disappeared, Benny and Louise talked for nearly two hours. He didn't want to leave. He talked over the whole Thames sacking again. Every detail of how he had been fêted in Cannes – the suite, the flowers, the limo – and then dumped so soon afterwards, was as fresh in his mind as if it had happened the day before. Louise told him: 'The press really love you again now.' Benny smiled. 'I know they do.'

At 7 p.m., the bell rang to warn that the evening performance was due to start in half an hour, and Benny realized he must reluctantly tear himself away. 'I suppose I'd better be going, little heart,' he said. Louise cried when he left. 'I could just see something terrible in his face. He looked very ill.'

Dennis Kirkland spoke to Benny on the Friday, and rang several times over the weekend but got no reply. He assumed that Benny had pottered off for one of his walks. Benny's last outing was to a shop in Teddington High Street where he bought food and some low-calorie drinks, probably on Saturday.

On Sunday, the news broke that Frankie Howerd, also by coincidence under contract to Central TV, had died at his home. The *Daily Mail* rang Kirkland to ask for a quote from Benny. Dennis, still not having been able to raise Benny, obligingly made one up about how upset Benny felt at the news. It was the sort of thing press agents do all the time. But Benny was already dead. It was the final irony. The last public utterance of a man who so hated being misquoted was something he could not possibly have said.

Epilogue

Benny's death dominated the papers for several days. The obituaries were fulsome, as if the press were trying to make amends, too late, for some of the things they had written about him three or four years earlier. Bob Hope and Michael Jackson paid tribute as well as Benny's peers in British showbusiness. On the following Tuesday evening, Thames dropped the Benny Hill compilation that was due to be screened, and showed a half-hour tribute instead. John Howard Davies diplomatically stepped back and let his former boss Philip Jones take charge. Sue Upton arrived at the studio sobbing so hard they thought she wouldn't be able to take part, but she pulled herself together in time. At the Adelphi Theatre, Louise English went on with the show like the professional Benny had brought her up to be. It was several weeks before she could bear to speak about what had happened.

Reporters in the British tabloids searched their files for the last mention of money in Benny's press cuttings, and turned up the story where Benny had allegedly said he would make Netta and Phoebe his main beneficiaries. Having established that Netta had died in February, they descended en masse on Phoebe King, then in a nursing home following her accident.

A full complement of reporters and photographers hot on a story is a daunting experience for anyone to have to face, never mind the unworldly Phoebe. Carried away by their attentions, she allowed herself to exaggerate slightly, and hinted that the ring Benny had given her had been worn on the third finger of her left hand, with his agreement.

Some of the papers next day referred to her as 'Benny's secret love'. Later, when the pack had departed, the truth hit her – her moment of fame and glory had only happened because Benny had died. She was overwhelmed with grief.

When Benny's will was eventually published several weeks later, it was the one that had been made in 1961. No later will was found. It left everything to his parents. His former accountant, who was named as executor, had to come out of retirement to deal with the estate, which would automatically go to the descendants of Benny's brother Leonard and his sister Diana, five nephews and nieces.

The funeral was held at Hollybrook Cemetery, Southampton, on 28 April, in the small chapel only a few feet from Benny's parents' grave.

His few relatives had hoped to keep it private and made all the arrangements at the undertakers in the name of Mr Alfred Hawthorne. But everyone found out and turned up anyway. His old school friends had their reunion after all – at the funeral. The people of Southampton lined the streets. Louise English noticed a small child doing a Fred Scuttle salute as the cortège drove by. It was a beautiful day at first, but as the mourners left the chapel and walked the few feet over to the Hill family grave, the heavens wept and everyone got soaked to the skin.

Bob Todd had set out from his home in Sussex to go first to London to pick up a dark suit at Moss Bros, then to Maidenhead to meet Henry McGee and Jon Jon Keefe. They would all travel to Southampton together from Jon Jon's home. First he got stuck in the traffic, then Moss Bros couldn't find a suit to fit him, then he went to the wrong platform at Paddington. As he neared Maidenhead with seconds to spare before the others had to leave, the train pulled up at some signals. And stayed there. They went without him. Toddy had a little weep because he had let everyone down, and then went to a pub instead. Benny would have roared with laughter.

Richard Stone was in California on the day of the funeral. He couldn't come to England because it was his golden wedding day, and his relatives were arriving from all over the world. They had booked rooms in a hotel for a huge family celebration. At some point, Richard's son gave him the videotape and Richard played it in the hotel bedroom. He suddenly came to the shots of Benny in bed at the hospital. 'I was very, very shocked and upset,' he said.

In Montreux the next day, Central TV's planned press lunch went ahead without any mention of the announcement they had hoped to make. The journalists just regarded it as one of the free meals of which they are so fond. Few people realized why Richard Holloway seemed a bit subdued.

While it awaits the return of the headstone with Benny's name added to those of his parents, Benny's grave has been tended by an old friend. She has brought fresh flowers nearly every day and planted pink and white alyssum so that it spells out his name: BENNY.